Cookies
from Many Lands

Cookies
from Many Lands

By
JOSEPHINE PERRY

DOVER PUBLICATIONS, INC.
NEW YORK

Published in Canada by General Publishing Company, Ltd., 30 Lesmill Road, Don Mills, Toronto, Ontario.
Published in the United Kingdom by Constable and Company, Ltd., 10 Orange Street, London WC 2.

This Dover edition, first published in 1972, is an unabridged and unaltered republication of the work first published in 1940 by M. Barrows, Inc., under the title *Around the World Making Cookies*.

International Standard Book Number: 0-486-22832-0
Library of Congress Catalog Card Number: 76-188953

Manufactured in the United States of America
Dover Publications, Inc.
180 Varick Street
New York, N. Y. 10014

To

the memory of my
Grandmothers

INTRODUCTION

COOKIES FROM MANY LANDS is the outgrowth of a hobby which began in my childhood and lasted through twenty years.

I loved the attic better than any room in the old house in the South where I was reared. Evidently my great-grandmother had the same fondness for it. She hoarded valuables in that attic. Her recipes, in a hand-written cook book, which I found in the attic, began my hobby for collecting formulas for small cakes. The interesting information she had written about the cakes was the inspiration for writing this book.

The collector's demand for nothing but the authentic grew in me as the years passed. No formula went into my collection unless it was the *best of its kind*. Gradually I began looking to other lands to satisfy my desire for new and unusual recipes. I found them in out of the way places, in cottages, in manor houses, in castles. I present them to the housewives around the world, with the hope that they may find as much pleasure in using them as I have found in collecting them and writing this book.

J. P.

TABLE OF CONTENTS

PART I

Page

CHOOSING THE RIGHT COOKIE

For Afternoon Tea

Almond Macaroons, 66; Almond Short Bread, 98; Almond Wafers, 56; Black Cake, 22; Chess Cakes, 15; Cinnamon Nut Meringues, 65; Cocoanut Balls, 67; Cocoanut Pralines, 48; Date Strips, 62; Haselnuss Makronen (Hazelnut Macaroons), 103; Hot Butter Tea Cakes, 18; Mandel Kränze (Almond Tea Cakes), 100; Orange Wafers, 54; Platzen (Drop Sponge Cakes), 115; Ring Tea Cakes, 20; Shrewsbury Cakes, 10; Tavern Biscuit, 10; Wafers, 13; Zimmt Sterne (Cinnamon Stars), 107.

For Parties

Hoide Kager (Overnight Cookies), 118; Berlinerkranzer (Egg Cakes), 126; Bertines Mandelbund (Almond Cakes), 127; Black Walnut Torte, 73; Chaux au Chocolat (Chocolate Cream Puffs), 81; Chocolate Pecan Cookies, 64; Chocolate Torte, 70; Cocoanut Macaroons, 67; Macaroons, 11; Orange Torte, 72; Pecan Cakes, 47; Pecan Macaroons, 66.

For Dessert with Fruit, Ice Cream, Etc.

American Short Bread, 52; Butter Cakes, 34; Hard Sugar Biscuit, 21; Hot Syrup Sponge Cake, 38; Lady Fingers, 68; Little Cakes to Ice, 91; Nut Meringues, 65; Plain Jumbles, 56; Plain Meringues, 64; Platzen (Drop Sponge Cakes), 115; Pound Cake, 98; Scotch Short Bread, 42; Sugar Cookies, 20; Vanilla Wafers, 54; Virginia Cookies, 12.

For Lunch Baskets

Banbury Cakes, 90; Butterscotch Cakes, 51; Butterscotch Cookies, 51; Card Gingerbread, 53; Cinnamon Fruit Cookies, 57; Date Drops, 62; Fried Jumbles, 57; Fruit Oatmeal Cookies, 32; Fruit Snaps, 37; Ginger Snaps, 26; Hard Fruit and Nut Cookies, 61; Honey Cakes, 22; Molasses Drop Cookies, 43.

For the Children's Cookie Jar

Aunt Cinny's Ginger Cakes, 14; Filled Cookies, 59; Flat Cakes, 34; Fruit Drop Cookies, 60; Ginger Cakes, 14; Hard Gingerbread, 25; Little Currant Cakes, 34; Oatmeal Cookies, 32; Overnight Gingerbread, 50; Raisin Cookies, 61; Soft Sugar Cookies, 44; Sour Cream Cookies, 35; Wild Honey Cakes, 21.

For Christmas

Anisplätzchen (Anise Seed Cakes), 108; Beaten Biscuit, 17; Black Walnut Cakes, 37; Brown Sugar Short Bread, 53; Butter Cookies, 52; Christmas Fruit Cookies, 59; Clabber Cake, 46; Cocoanut Chess Cakes, 16; Coffee Ginger Cakes, 26; Creole Cocoanut Macaroons, 46; Crullers, 24; French Fruit Cookies, 46; Fruit Cookies, 31; Little Fruit Cakes, 31; Little Plum Cakes, 13; Mandel Bretzel (Almond Pretzel), 106; Mandel Kränze (Almond Tea Cakes), 100; Mandel Strangen (Almond Strips), 102; Scotch Ginger Cake, 95; Small Fruit Cakes, 30; Walnut Cookies, 63.

For Summer

Arrowroot Cakes, 42; Cream Tea Cakes, 19; Gâteaux Chambord (Sponge Cake), 82; Meringués à la Crème (Cream Meringues), 80; Rout Cakes, 90; Sour Cream Ginger Cake, 95; Sugar Biscuit, 20; Water Cakes, 9.

For Gift Boxes

Almond Short Bread, 98; Beaten Biscuit, 17; Black Walnut Cake, 37; Black Cake, 22; Caraway Cake, 29; Cocoanut Balls, 67; Cocoanut Pralines, 48; Date Strips, 62; Leb Küchen (Honey Cakes), 108; Makronen (Cocoanut Macaroons), 106; Mandel Kränze (Almond Tea Cakes), 100; Peanut Wafers, 55; Pound Cake, 98; Rich Ginger Cake, 92; Seed Cakes, 28; Virginia Cookies, 12; Weise Pfeffernüsse (White Peppernuts), 109; Zimmt Sterne (Cinnamon Stars), 107.

WHAT KIND OF COOKIES SHALL I BAKE?

Buttermilk or Sour Milk

Pages 25, 32, 33, 41, 44, 56, 95, 96, 122

Cheese Cakes

Pages 85, 113, 137, 140

Chess Cakes

Pages 15, 16

Chocolate

Pages 36, 64, 70, 81, 102, 112

Cocoanut

Pages 16, 45, 46, 48, 56, 67, 69, 106, 151

Cookies That Will Keep

Pages 9, 12, 14, 15, 26, 35, 41, 51, 61, 62, 105

Cream Cookies

Pages 9, 19, 23, 34, 56, 58, 80, 85, 93, 97, 113, 118, 120, 122, 123, 126

Sour Cream

Pages 27, 35, 46, 95, 138

Fat (Without)

Pages 30, 34, 36, 55, 62, 63, 67, 68, 82, 84, 90, 94, 96, 101, 102, 103, 104, 106, 107, 108, 109, 142, 145

Fruit Cookies

Pages 13, 22, 24, 29, 30, 31, 32, 33, 34, 37, 46, 50, 57, 58, 59, 60, 61, 62, 71, 73, 83, 84, 86, 90, 92, 95, 96, 105, 108, 109, 114, 131, 146

Honey Cakes

Pages 21, 50, 108, 140

Ice Box Cookies

Pages 50, 51, 52, 117, 118, 120, 121

Lard

Pages 26, 33, 36, 40, 44, 53, 54, 105, 107

PART I

Cookie Making in America
Colonial Times to the Present Day

CONTENTS

COOKERY AMERICANA

THE MELTING pot that has taken people from many lands and fused them into our sturdy American stock has been just as busy evolving a typical American cookery.

American cookery had its greatest influence at first from English, Scotch and Dutch cooking as it was practiced in the early seventeenth century. Then came the French influence to put its stamp upon some localities, New Orleans for example, but to make no appreciable change upon the trend cooking was taking naturally.

Virginia and New England followed the English type of culinary art. But early in the history in these two sections of Colonial America there were developed definite differences in cookery because of climatic conditions and modes of living.

Scotch cookery flourished in all sections of Colonial America. Wherever there was a Scotchman there was also cake made of oatmeal and treacle. Scotch cookery can be placed in no special locality in America, but its place of importance in Cookery Americana is unquestioned by the student of culinary art as it is practiced by the modern American housewife.

Dutch cookery came to New York and Pennsylvania and stayed. The *gemberkoek* of colonial days is the ginger cake of today. Good old Dutch cookery, like good old Scotch cookery, was *sound, simple* food. *Sound, simple* food met the physical needs of a pioneer people, who had to face and overcome hardships in a New World, before any distinctive national culture could be evolved. Modern American cookery is characterized by those old Colonial necessities, *soundness* and *simplicity* of food.

The modern American woman approaches all questions of food from the standpoint of quality. She demands the best, the freshest, the most carefully handled food product, for her money. Every alert American woman is an authority on the quality of food. Housewives, not food experts, have succeeded in evolving a Cookery Americana, which has at last brought Old World recognition of the excellence of American food.

The present day traveler from the United States is not made to feel, as he was in the eighties and nineties, that he should be apologetic for the lack his homeland suffered in culinary art. Instead he is apologized to. People of other lands, especially if they are widely traveled, are beginning to evaluate food as Americans do. That evolution is based on a nice blending of scientific principles with gastronomic pleasures and recognizes the soundness of the American woman's demands for fresh foods, handled in the most sanitary way. So America takes her place in world cookery. And it is an honored place.

As we go AROUND THE WORLD MAKING COOKIES it is fitting that the evolution of American cookie making, from colonial times to the present day, be given first consideration. Then other countries, especially those noted for small cake making, will contribute their choice formulas, rounding out the collection of small cake recipes gathered from many lands.

COOKIE MAKING MADE EASY

BAKING is as important as making, if perfect small cakes are desired.

Ovens differ. Use the various temperatures given in the recipes as a guide. But perfect your own baking temperatures, according to the best results obtained from your oven.

In using an electric oven, after the oven registers the correct heat, turn the top element off. Bake with the top element turned off.

Use block tin baking sheets for the best results. The pans should not touch the walls of the oven. Most cookies burn easily. Especially is this true of cookies made of molasses and cookies made with no milk. Cookies must be watched constantly. Turn the pans frequently, while baking, to insure even browning. If you are not experienced do not start baking until all the cookies are on the baking sheets.

Grease the pans with butter. This gives the good buttery taste that is necessary for choice cookies. Place the cookies on the pans, allowing space for them to spread.

After each pan of cookies is baked wipe off the baking sheet with a piece of heavy brown paper, slightly greased. Washing the pans between bakings has a tendency to cause cakes to stick. This is particularly true of rolled cookies.

Never put a cookie on a hot pan. Never pile the cookies on top of each other to cool. Cool on sheets of brown paper.

The American method of baking is *quick baking*. The cookies are not allowed to dry out. For quick baking put the cookies into a 450° F. oven and reduce the temperature as needed. If hard cookies are desired, after the cookies are baked the temperature is reduced to 250° F. and the cakes are allowed to stay in the oven to dry out.

The Northern European method of baking is *slow baking*. This makes a crisper harder cookie. The temperatures should be 350° F. to 275° F.

Measure accurately. Use standard cup and spoon measures.

Always measure flour before sifting unless the recipe says: measure after sifting. The amount varies several tablespoonfuls before and after sifting.

Measuring the fat is important for the best results. Cutters are on the market to cut pound cakes of butter or lard into cupfuls or portions of cupfuls. These are convenient as a labor saver, as well as a means of accurate measurement.

Pastry blenders are also on the market. These are particularly useful in blending butter into flour and sugar, in cookie making. The use of the blender prevents the fat from becoming oily, as it frequently does when the blending is done with the hands.

A large rubber plate scraper, with flexible points, is an indispensable kitchen implement in cookie making. Use the scraper for removing mixed ingredients from bowls. It prevents waste and insures accuracy.

An approximate estimate of the number of cookies a recipe makes is arrived at by the amount of flour used. For example, Virginia Cookies, calling for one and one-half cups of flour makes about thirty cakes the size of a twenty-five cent piece.

CAKE MAKING IN VIRGINIA

Gingerbread Cakes

Sift together

10 cups flour
2 tbsp. ginger
1 nutmeg grated
½ tsp. salt

2 cups butter
2 cups sugar
1 cup molasses
½ cup cream

Blend the butter into the flour. Heat the molasses, sugar and cream together. Add the hot liquid to the flour. Knead to a smooth stiff dough. Roll thin and cut into large round cakes. Bake at 400° F. for about eight minutes.

Water Cakes

This is a favorite Virginia recipe, of English origin, used since colonial times. We still find these cakes served for Tea in many Southern homes whose mistresses pride themselves upon their culinary ability.

Sift together

10 cups flour
2 cups sugar

2 cups butter
1½ cups milk boiling hot
2 tbsp. caraway seed

Blend the butter into the flour until the mixture is mealy. Add the caraway seed. Mix into a dough with the milk. Roll very thin and cut into cakes the size of a saucer. Prick full of holes with a fork. Bake at 350° F. until light brown. These cookies keep well.

Shrewsbury Cakes

This cookie recipe came to America with our first grand-mothers, back in the days when English gentlemen were sent to colonial Virginia to sit in the House of Burgesses.

One day, if luck smiles upon you, you will drop into a mountain cabin in North Carolina and a venerable grand-mother will serve you a cup of tea poured from an ancient silver pot. Then she will bring out little tea biscuits, which she still calls Shrewsbury cakes, and which she still makes by her famous old recipe.

Sift together

8 cups flour	½ cup milk
2 cups sugar	1½ cups butter melted
1 tbsp. coriander seed powdered	6 eggs unbeaten

Add the butter, milk and eggs to the flour. Mix well and knead to a smooth dough. Roll very thin, cut into small shapes and bake at 400° F. until light brown.

Tavern Biscuit

Virginia has many old English recipes which have been cherished along with her other traditions. Tavern Biscuits still have a special place on the Afternoon Tea menu in many a plantation house.

Sift together

4 cups flour	1¼ cups milk
½ tsp. nutmeg	1 cup sugar
1 cup butter	½ tsp. mace

Blend the butter and flour together until the mixture is mealy. Gradually add the milk and knead into a smooth dough. Roll thin and cut into small round shapes. Bake at 450° F. until light brown.

Drop Tea Biscuit

Sift together five times

3 cups flour
½ tsp. salt

Sift three times
2 cups sugar

8 eggs beaten ten minutes

Add the sugar and flour alternately to the eggs, folding them in lightly. Drop into small cookies. Bake at 325° F. for ten to fifteen minutes.

Macaroons

1 lb. powdered sugar sifted
7 egg whites beaten dry

2 tbsp. rose water
1 lb. almonds blanched

Put the almonds in the refrigerator three hours before using. This prevents oiliness. Roll them on a biscuit board or marble slab until they are finely powdered. Add the rose water gradually to the almonds blending the mixture well. Gradually add the sugar to the egg whites. When all the sugar is added mix in the almonds. Drop into small cookies. Bake at 250° F. for thirty minutes.

Afternoon Tea Cakes

Mix

4 cups flour sifted
1⅓ cups brown sugar

½ cup butter
½ cup milk

Melt the butter in the milk, being careful that it does not boil. Mix the milk into the flour and knead thoroughly. The dough must be smooth and light. Roll thin and cut into strips one inch wide and three inches long. Bake slowly on a griddle. The griddle does not need greasing.

Jumbles

Sift together

8 cups flour
2 cups sugar
1 tsp. mace
1 tsp. cloves
½ tsp. cinnamon

1½ cups butter melted
4 eggs beaten ten minutes

Pour the eggs and butter into the flour and mix well. Knead until the dough is smooth and does not stick to the hands. Form into little rings with the hands. Bake at 400° F. for ten to twelve minutes. These cookies keep well for several weeks if kept in a well-covered crock.

Virginia Cookies

The story is commonly told in Virginia that these cookies were a favorite with Dolly Madison. They were the dainty confection served with syllabub, the favorite dessert in those days. And syllabub, the venerable grandmother in the mountain cabin in North Carolina, will tell you, was a mixture of calf's foot jelly and whipped cream. The jelly was made with wine.

1½ cups flour sifted
½ cup powdered sugar sifted
almonds blanched

2 egg yolks unbeaten
½ cup butter

Cream the butter and sugar together. Add the egg yolks and mix well. Gradually add the flour and knead into a smooth dough. Shape into small balls with the hands. Press an almond into the top of each cookie, and bake about twenty minutes at 400° F.

Little Plum Cakes

4 cups flour sifted
1 lb. powdered sugar sifted
1 lb. butter unsalted
1 lb. currants
1 lb. raisins

1 tsp. nutmeg
rind of 1 lemon grated
12 eggs unbeaten
3 tbsp. milk

Mix one cup of flour with the fruit. Cream the butter until soft. Add the lemon rind and nutmeg. Add the flour, sugar and eggs alternately. Lastly mix in the fruit. Drop into small cookies. Bake at 450° F. until brown then reduce the heat to 350° F. and finish baking.

Wafers

Wafer irons were in every well furnished kitchen in colonial America. They were mentioned as being one of the culinary necessities in English households in the early sixteenth century. They ceased to be used by many housewives when copper pots were discarded for modern equipment. But wafer irons are coming back into fashion.

2 cups flour sifted 3 times
$\frac{1}{2}$ cup butter melted
6 eggs beaten ten minutes

$\frac{1}{2}$ cup sugar
$\frac{1}{2}$ cup milk

Add the sugar gradually to the eggs. Add the flour and milk alternately, stirring the batter as little as possible. Bake quickly in the wafer iron. Roll while hot.

Ginger Cakes

What Southern child does not remember, with a little thrill, the ginger cakes? It was a special ginger cake, baked in a special way and kept in large stone crocks, year in and year out.

Sift together

12 cups flour
1 tbsp. ginger
1 tsp. cloves
1 tsp. salt

1 cup butter
2 cups brown sugar
1 cup thick molasses

Put the butter and molasses in a sauce pan and set it on a warm place on the stove so the butter will melt slowly. Mix the sugar with the flour. Add the molasses gradually to the flour and knead the dough for ten minutes. Roll into thin sheets. Fit the sheets into well greased baking pans and mark into squares, using a floured knife. Bake at 350° F. for about thirty minutes. Break the cookies apart while they are still warm. The lack of soda makes the cookies hard and increases their keeping qualities. They will keep for weeks.

Aunt Cinny's Ginger Cakes

The South has always had its famous negro cooks. The art of cooking is handed down from mother to daughter, from one generation to the next.

Aunt Cinny, the cook in the author's great-grandmother's household, was noted in her day. Her praises are still sung in many old families of Virginia, who pride themselves on real Southern dishes.

Sift together

8 cups flour	2 cups sugar
3 tsp. soda	2 cups molasses
1 tsp. salt	1 lb. butter creamed
1 tbsp. Jamaica ginger	3 tbsp. vinegar
	6 eggs beaten ten minutes

Add the sugar, eggs, molasses and vinegar gradually to the butter and mix well. Pour the mixture into the flour and knead the dough until it does not stick to the hands. Roll to one-eighth inch thickness. Cut into large square cakes. Bake at 400° F. until light brown. These cakes keep well.

Chess Cakes

No list of old Southern recipes is complete without Chess Cakes. Chess Cakes are as common for afternoon tea in such communities as Alexandria, Virginia, as currant buns are on the English tea table. These cakes are a dainty confection no bigger than a silver dollar.

1 cup sugar	4 egg yolks
$\frac{1}{8}$ cup butter	1 egg

Cream the butter until soft enough to mix with the sugar. Add the eggs and mix until the egg ceases to be stringy. Line small tart shells with pastry rolled paper thin. Put a small spoon of the filling in each tart shell. Bake at 450° F. until the pastry is set. Reduce the heat to 350° F. and finish baking.

Citron Chess Cakes

3 eggs	3 cups sugar
$\frac{1}{2}$ cup butter	citron cut in thin pieces

Cut the butter into small cubes. Mix it with the sugar and eggs and stir five minutes. Heat slowly, stirring constantly. When the mixture begins to thicken remove from the fire. Put a layer of citron in the bottom of tart shells which have been lined with pastry. Put in a small spoon of the filling. To bake, follow the directions given for Chess Cakes.

These chess cakes may be varied by jam, fruit or nuts, candied orange peel or candied ginger used instead of citron.

Cocoanut Chess Cakes

1½ cups cocoanut   1⅓ cups water
2 cups sugar   ½ cup butter
7 egg yolks well beaten

Boil the sugar and water together to the soft ball stage. Stir in the cocoanut and continue boiling and stirring for fifteen minutes. Remove from the fire and add the butter, stirring until it is melted. Add the eggs gradually. Bake as directed for Chess Cakes.

Colonial Chess Cakes

This is one of the oldest of the many Chess Cake recipes. It was a favorite with colonial housewives. They served it hot for special dinners. They made it into tiny cakes for parties. They varied it to suit their individual fancy, by adding candied fruits and different kinds of nuts.

1 cup sugar   ½ nutmeg grated
1 cup butter melted   ⅛ tsp. salt
8 eggs beaten 10 minutes

Add the butter, sugar, salt and nutmeg to the eggs and mix well. Place the bowl in a pan of simmering water and cook, stirring constantly, until the mixture begins to thicken. Bake as directed for Chess Cakes.

Puff Paste

No Virginia housewife thinks of making Chess Cakes without real puff paste. It is more trouble than ordinary pastry but it is worth the time and effort used.

Sift together

2 cups flour	1 cup butter
½ tsp. salt	⅓ cup ice water

Work the butter until it is smooth and flexible. Shape into a flat square cake and place on ice until ready to use. Mix the water into the flour and knead the dough for ten minutes. Roll the dough in a napkin and place on ice for fifteen minutes. Roll the paste in a square shape. Place the butter in the center, fold the dough over the butter and roll thin. Repeat the folding and rolling process six times.

The dough must not be allowed to soften. Place it in the ice box when signs of softening occur. Usually it can be rolled twice each time before returning it to the ice box. The dough must be thoroughly chilled before using.

Beaten Biscuit

In some of the very old cook books these delectable little biscuits are called "Apoquiniminc Cakes." They are typically Southern, and are still an everyday food in many households, in spite of the time and energy required in making them.

Sift together

4 cups flour
½ tsp. salt

1½ cups milk
½ cup butter
1 egg well beaten

Blend the butter into the flour until the mixture is mealy. Gradually add the milk and egg and knead into a smooth dough. Beat the dough with a pestle for thirty minutes. It will be bubbly and light when it is beaten enough. Roll thin and cut into small cakes. Bake at 450° F. for fifteen minutes.

These cakes were baked on a griddle in colonial times.

Hot Butter Tea Cakes

Many of the choicest colonial recipes for small cakes were given no special name. They were called Tea Cakes. Many Southern housewives still prefer calling their cookies Tea Cakes, just as they prefer some of the recipes their grandmothers used to modern formulas calling for baking powder.

Hot Butter Tea Cakes is a recipe from the Winston family of Virginia. It is so old no one knows just how it came to America. But the story was told by the author's great-grandmother that Winston women were famous for their beauty and their ability as housewives. There were seven famous Winston sisters, the daughters of a Virginia gentleman who was important in shaping the laws, the customs, the ideals of America in his day. His seven daughters became just as important in shaping the culinary traditions of their descendants. Dolly Madison was a descendant of one of the famous Winston sisters. When she was mistress of the White House she used the Tea

Cake recipe and increased its fame. That fame lasts to this day.

4 cups flour sifted   2 cups sugar
1 cup butter   3 eggs unbeaten

Melt the butter slowly by setting it into a pot of simmering water. Allow the butter to remain in the water until it is very hot. Pour the hot butter over the flour, mixing thoroughly as it is poured in. Add the sugar and mix well. Add the eggs one at a time and mix into a smooth dough. Roll thin and cut into small cakes. Bake at 400° F. until light brown.

Cream Tea Cakes

These Tea Cakes are popular in many Southern homes. You will notice that many of the old recipes had no flavoring. The delectable buttery taste was considered sufficient flavor.

In baking these cakes it is important to do all the greasing of pans with butter. That accentuates the buttery taste.

Sift together
5 cups flour   3 cups sugar
½ tsp. soda   1 cup butter
                             1 cup cream
                             3 eggs unbeaten

Cream the butter and sugar together. Add the eggs, one at a time and mix well. Add the flour and cream alternately. Knead to a smooth dough, adding more flour if needed. Roll thin and cut into large round cakes. Bake at 400° F. until light brown.

Ring Tea Cakes

Sift five times

1½ cups flour

1 cup sugar
¼ tsp. almond extract
4 eggs beaten ten minutes

Gradually add the sugar to the eggs. Add the flavoring. Add the flour a little at a time, folding it in lightly. Drop into small cookies. Bake at 325° F. for about ten minutes. Remove from the pan carefully and bring the edges of the cake over each other, forming a ring.

Sugar Cookies

Sift together

3 cups flour
1 tsp. soda

1½ cups sugar
1 cup butter
4 eggs unbeaten

Cream the butter and sugar together. Add the eggs, one at a time, and mix well. Add the flour gradually and knead into a soft dough. Roll thin, cut into small round shapes and sprinkle with sugar. Bake at 400° F. for eight to ten minutes.

Sugar Biscuit

Sift together

6 cups flour
¼ tsp. salt

1½ cups sugar
1½ cups butter
2 tbsp. rose water
4 eggs beaten ten minutes

Cream the butter and sugar together until very light. Add the rose water and eggs and mix well. Add the flour gradually and knead into a smooth dough. Roll thin, cut into small round cakes and bake at 400° F. until light brown.

Hard Sugar Biscuit

Sift together

4 cups flour	1 cup sugar
½ tsp. soda	1 cup butter
1½ tsp. cinnamon	¾ cup milk
	1 tsp. caraway seed

Dissolve the sugar in the milk. Blend the butter into the flour and mix in the caraway seed. Add the milk gradually to the flour and knead into a smooth dough. Roll to one-half inch thickness, cut into small biscuits, prick with a fork and bake at 450° F. for twelve to fifteen minutes.

Wild Honey Cakes

Wild honey is dark in color and very highly flavored. Southern housewives still use wild honey, if they can get it, and if they can not they purchase Guatamala honey. It is quite like the Southern wild honey that has a suggestive flavor of jasmine.

Sift together

5 cups flour	2 cups honey
1 tsp. salt	1 cup butter
2 tbsp. Jamaica ginger	3 tsp. soda

Bring the honey and butter to a boil and then cool. Add the soda and beat until it foams. Pour the honey mixture into the flour and mix well. Knead the dough until it does

not stick to the hands.   Roll thin and cut into small cakes.
Bakes at 400° F. until light brown.

Honey Cakes

¼ lb. citron sliced thin
¼ lb. candied orange peel
  sliced thin
1 cup honey warmed
2 eggs well beaten

3 cups flour sifted
1 cup sugar
½ cup butter creamed

Pour the honey over the citron and orange peel and let
it stand over night.   Add the sugar and butter to the eggs
and beat thoroughly.   Mix with the fruit and honey.
Gradually add the flour and knead into a smooth dough.
Roll thin and cut into small round cakes.   Bake at 400° F.
for about ten minutes.

Black Cake

Black Cake was the colonial name for Fruit Cake.   This
recipe was sent to the author with the following note:

> This cake was a favorite in the household of
> Mrs. Dearborn, wife of General Henry Dearborn,
> who was Secretary of War during Thomas Jeffer-
> son's administration, and who was sent by Presi-
> dent Jefferson to West Point to establish the
> Military Academy.
>
> It was a custom with mother and grandmother
> to fourth the recipe and bake the cake in a shallow
> pan.   They dredged the cake over with flour while
> it was warm then wiped the flour off carefully
> before spreading on a plain icing.   It was then cut
> in little strips and served for Afternoon Tea.

2 lbs. flour sifted (about 8 cups)
2 lbs. butter
8 lbs. currants washed and dried thoroughly
6 lbs. seeded raisins
2 lbs. citron sliced thin

2 lbs. brown sugar (4 cups, generous measure)
1 cup wine
1 cup brandy
1 tbsp. each: mace, cinnamon, nutmeg and cloves
18 eggs beaten until foamy

Blend the butter, sugar, spices and six cups of flour together until the mixture is mealy. Mix the rest of the flour with the fruit. Add the eggs to the first mixture and gradually add the fruit, alternating it with the wine and brandy.

Line pans with heavy brown paper. Grease well. Turn the batter into the pans and bake at 350° F. for two to three hours.

Grandma Hopkin's Favorite Tea Cakes

Many of the oldest recipes call for soda, with no acid to neutralize it. They are different and worth trying

Sift together

2 cups flour
1 tsp. soda

1 cup butter
3 cups sugar
1 cup thick cream
4 eggs unbeaten
flour sifted

Mix the butter and sugar until blended but not creamed. Add the eggs and mix lightly. Add the cream. Stir this mixture into the two cups of flour and then add enough flour to make a dough that will roll. Use as little flour as possible. Roll the dough thick, cut into large squares and bake at 400° F. until light brown.

"Derby" Cakes

8 cups flour sifted	2 cups butter
1 lb. currants	1 cup milk
1 lb. moist brown sugar	1 egg well beaten

Blend the butter into the flour until the mixture is mealy. Add the currants and sugar and mix well. Mix into a smooth dough with the milk and egg. Roll thin, cut into round cakes and bake at 400° F. until light brown.

Newport Egg Biscuit

Sift together

2 cups flour	3 eggs unbeaten
$\frac{1}{2}$ tsp. salt	

Pour the eggs into the flour and mix into a stiff dough. Beat with a pestle or steak beater until the dough begins to blister. Roll very thin. Cut into small round biscuits and fry in boiling fat. Drain on brown paper. Sprinkle with salt.

These biscuits are served with orange marmalade for Afternoon Tea.

Crullers

Sift together	Mix together
2 cups flour	4 tbsp. milk·
1 tsp. salt	1 tsp. soda
1 nutmeg grated	4 tbsp. butter melted
	6 tbsp. sugar
	4 eggs unbeaten

Mix the sugar, eggs and butter together until thoroughly blended. Mix in the flour, adding more if needed to make a soft dough. Roll thin, cut into small biscuits and fry to a golden brown in boiling fat. Drain on brown paper and roll in sugar.

NEW ENGLAND RECIPES

New England and Virginia were settled by the same stock from England. The old recipes that follow are found especially in New England households that have cherished their best colonial traditions. Many of them are known equally well by Southern housewives. And in any community in America, if one will take the time to look, one will find an excellent housekeeper who prides herself upon her cleverness as a cook, and particularly takes pride in cookie baking day. Then she gets out cookie recipes brought across the plains by a grandmother who prized her *family cooking secrets* as much as she did the *hollow gold* breast pin with the onyx inlay, or the old sampler with the date 1784 worked into the corner.

Hard Ginger Bread

6 cups flour sifted
1 tsp. cloves
rind of 1 lemon grated
2 tbsp. Jamaica ginger

2 cups dark molasses warmed
1 cup butter
1 cup buttermilk
1 tbsp. soda

Cut the butter into small pieces and melt it in the molasses. Add the buttermilk, spices, lemon rind and soda and mix well. Pour the molasses mixture over the flour and mix into a smooth dough, adding more flour if needed. Roll into thin sheets, dust with powdered sugar and bake at 400° F. until light brown. Cut into large squares while still warm.

Coffee Ginger Cakes

Sift together

5 cups flour	2 cups sugar
1 tsp. salt	1 cup butter
2 tsp. ginger	1 cup New Orleans molasses
Dissolve	1 egg well beaten
3 tsp. soda	2 tsp. vanilla
1 cup strong hot coffee	

Mix the butter, sugar, molasses and hot coffee and stir until the butter is melted. Allow to cool then add the egg and vanilla. Gradually add the flour and mix into a soft dough. Roll thick and cut into large round cakes. Bake at 400° F. ten to fifteen minutes.

Ginger Snaps

New England ginger snaps have been famous for many generations. The story is told that the first commercial ginger snaps baked and sold in a public bakery in America were made from a recipe furnished by a housewife in Roxbury, Massachusetts.

Sift together

3 cups flour	1 cup molasses
1 tbsp. ginger	½ cup sugar
1 tsp. salt	½ cup butter
	¼ cup lard

Cream the fat and sugar together. Add the molasses and mix well. Gradually add the flour and knead to a smooth dough. Roll thin and cut into three-inch squares. Bake at 400° F. until light brown. These cakes keep well.

Dark Ginger Snaps

Sift together

6 cups flour	½ cup butter
1 tsp. cloves	½ cup lard
1 tbsp. Jamaica ginger	1 cup sugar
1 tsp. salt	1 cup dark molasses

Dissolve

1 tsp. soda
⅓ cup ice water

Cream the sugar and fat together. Add the molasses and water. Gradually mix in the flour and knead into a smooth dough. Roll thin, cut into small round cakes and bake at 400° F. until light brown.

Ginger Cookies

These cookies are a favorite in New Hampshire households where the women pride themselves upon the shine of their pots and pans and the excellence of their gingerbread. The recipe was passed along as a very special concession.

Sift together

5 cups flour	2 cups molasses
1½ tsp. soda	1 cup sugar
1 tsp. cinnamon	1 cup butter
1 tbsp. Jamaica ginger	1 cup sour cream
	2 eggs unbeaten

Cream the butter and sugar together. Add the eggs, one at a time and mix well. Add the molasses and the sour cream. Mix in the flour and knead into a smooth dough. Roll thin, cut into large cakes, sprinkle with sugar and bake at 350° F. until light brown.

Soft Ginger Cookies

Sift together

1½ cups flour
½ tsp. soda
¼ tsp. each: ginger and salt

1 cup butter
½ cup sugar
½ cup molasses
2 eggs well beaten

Cream the butter and sugar together. Stir in the eggs, flour and molasses. Knead into a soft dough. Roll one half inch thick. Place in a well greased baking pan and bake at 400° F. for about fifteen minutes. Cut into small squares while still warm.

Seed Cakes

Seed cakes were very popular in colonial America. The recipes were brought from England and were used both in New England and the Southern States. But during the Revolutionary period, when America had to do without most luxuries and many necessities, seed cakes became almost unknown, and they have never been commonly used since.

Sift together

8 cups flour
½ tsp. soda

1½ cups butter
2 cups sugar
1 cup milk
6 eggs unbeaten
1 tbsp. coriander seed

Cream the butter and sugar together. Add the coriander seed and the eggs and mix well. Add the flour and milk alternately and knead into a smooth dough. Roll thin, cut into large round cakes and bake at 450° F. until light brown.

Caraway Cakes

Sift together

8 cups flour	1 cup butter softened
1 tsp. soda	4 cups sugar
Add	1 cup milk
	2 eggs well beaten
1 cup caraway seed	1 tsp. lemon extract

Beat the butter, sugar and eggs together. Add the lemon extract. Add the flour and milk alternately and knead into a stiff, smooth dough. Roll thin, cut into large round cakes and bake at 400° F. until light brown.

Plum Cakes

Plum cakes were as popular in colonial New England as they were in England. These are the typical plum cakes of the past.

Sift together

4 cups flour	¾ cup butter
¼ tsp. mace	¾ cup sugar
½ tsp. allspice	3 eggs well beaten
Add	
1 lb. currants	

Cream the butter and sugar together. Add the eggs and mix well. Add all of the flour at once and stir up quickly. Drop into small cakes. Bake at 450° F. until light brown. Reduce the temperature to 350° F. and finish baking.

Raisin Cakes

Sift together

1 cup flour
1 tsp. soda

2 cups flour sifted
1 cup brown sugar
2 cups molasses
1 cup butter
1 cup raisins
1 tsp. salt
1 tsp. ginger
¼ tsp. nutmeg

Mix the butter, sugar and molasses together and heat slowly. Add the salt and spices and let come to a slow boil. Simmer for five minutes. Remove from the fire and gradually stir in two cups of flour. Add the raisins and the flour and soda and mix into a stiff dough. Drop into small cakes and bake at 400° F. until light brown. Reduce the temperature to 350° F. and finish baking.

Small Fruit Cakes

Sift together

3 cups flour
1 tsp. soda
2 tsp. cream of tartar
½ tsp. nutmeg
1 tsp. cloves
2 tsp. cinnamon

1 lb. brown sugar
¼ lb. citron cut thin
½ cup nuts chopped
4 eggs beaten ten minutes

Add the sugar, nuts and citron to the eggs and mix well. Fold in the flour, stirring it in as quickly as possible. Drop into small cakes and bake at 400° F. for ten to fifteen minutes.

Little Fruit Cakes

Sift together

2½ cups flour
1 tsp. mace
1 tsp. cloves
2 tsp. cinnamon
1 tsp. soda
1 tsp. cream of tartar

1 cup butter
2 cups brown sugar
2 cups raisins
1 cup black walnut meats
   chopped
3 eggs

Cream the butter, sugar and eggs together. Add the flour, nuts and raisins and stir up quickly. Drop into small cakes and bake at 450° F. ten to fifteen minutes.

Fruit Cookies

Sift together

4 cups flour
1 tsp. cinnamon
1 tsp. ginger

Mix with

1 cup raisins
1 cup currants
1 cup chopped nuts

1½ cups sugar
½ cup molasses
½ cup hot water
1 cup butter
3 eggs
1 tsp. soda

Cream the butter, sugar and eggs together until light. Mix the molasses, hot water and soda together and when it foams add it and the flour alternately to the butter mixture. Spread one inch thick in well buttered baking pans and bake at 350° F. for about thirty minutes. Cut into small squares when cold.

Fruit Oatmeal Cookies

Sift together

½ cup flour
½ tsp. salt
½ tsp. soda
1 tsp. cinnamon
½ tsp. cloves
½ tsp. mace

½ cup butter
1 cup sugar
1¾ cups oatmeal
5 tbsp. buttermilk
1 egg well beaten

Mix

1 cup flour
½ cup walnuts chopped
½ cup citron sliced
½ cup raisins chopped

Cream the butter and sugar together. Add the egg, buttermilk and one-half cup of flour and mix well. Add the oatmeal and mix well. Then add the fruit and blend in as lightly and quickly as possible. Drop into small cakes and bake at 450° F. until light brown. Reduce the temperature to 350° F. and finish baking.

Oatmeal Cookies

Sift together

2 cups flour
1 tsp. soda
1 tsp. salt
1 tsp. cinnamon

2 cups oatmeal
1 cup sugar
¾ cup butter softened
2 eggs unbeaten

Mix with

1 cup raisins chopped

Cream the butter, sugar and eggs together. Add half of the flour and mix well. Add all of the oatmeal and mix well. Add the remainder of the flour, mixing it in just enough to blend it in thoroughly. Drop into small cakes and bake at 400° F. for ten to fifteen minutes.

Soft Oatmeal Cookies

Sift together

4 cups flour
½ tsp. soda
1 tsp. nutmeg
1 tsp. salt

Mix with

½ lb. seeded raisins

3½ cups rolled oats
2 cups sugar
½ cup lard softened
1½ cups sour milk (buttermilk)
4 eggs

Cream the sugar, fat and eggs together. Add the milk and half of the flour alternately. Mix in all of the oatmeal. Add the remainder of the flour and mix in quickly. Drop into small cakes and bake at 450° F. for twelve to fifteen minutes.

Ground Oatmeal Cookies

Sift together

2 cups flour
½ tsp. salt
1 tsp. soda
½ tsp. nutmeg

2 cups rolled oats
1 cup butter
1 cup brown sugar
½ cup sour milk

Grind the rolled oats through the food chopper and mix with the flour. Cream the butter and sugar together until very light. Add the flour and milk alternately and knead into a soft dough. Roll thin, cut into large cakes and bake at 400° F. for ten to fifteen minutes.

Butter Cakes

Sift together

4 cups flour
1 tsp. cinnamon
1 tbsp. ginger
½ tsp. salt

1 cup butter
1½ cups soft brown sugar
2 eggs
grated rind of 2 lemons

Cream the butter and sugar together. Add the eggs, one at a time and beat until very light. Add the lemon rind. Gradually add the flour, kneading the dough until it is smooth. Roll thin, cut into small cakes and bake at 400° F. until light brown.

Little Currant Cakes

Mix together

1 egg well beaten
1 tbsp. rose water

cream

4 cups flour sifted
1 cup powdered sugar
    sifted
½ cup butter
1 cup currants
¼ tsp. nutmeg

Work the butter into the flour until the mixture is mealy. Add the powdered sugar and nutmeg. Mix the egg into the flour, adding cream as needed to make a smooth dough. Work in the currants. Roll medium thin, cut into small squares and bake at 400° F. until light brown.

Flat Cakes

Sift together

8 cups flour
2 cups sugar

Mix with

2 tbsp. caraway seed

Mix

4 eggs well beaten
3 tbsp. cold water
⅛ tsp. salt

Gradually add the egg mixture to the flour and knead into a stiff dough. Roll very thin, cut into large round cakes and bake at 400° F. until light brown.

While the cakes are baking boil 2 cups of sugar and 1 cup of water to the soft ball stage. Dip the hot cookies into the hot syrup and return them to the oven for five minutes. Turn off the heat and leave the cookies in the cooling oven to dry out.

These cakes will keep several weeks if put away in a tightly covered crock, and kept in a cool dry place.

Sour Cream Cookies

Farmwives of New England have always been famous for their sour cream cakes. This recipe is very old and very choice. It is from a hand-written cook book owned by a woman noted far and wide for her sour cream cakes.

Sift together

4 cups flour
½ tsp. salt
1 tsp. soda

1 cup butter
2 cups sugar
1 cup sour cream
2 eggs unbeaten
1 tsp. lemon extract

Cream the butter and sugar together. Add the eggs, one at a time and beat until light. Add the flavoring. Add the flour and cream alternately and mix into a soft dough. Handle the dough lightly while rolling it thin and cutting it into fancy shapes. Sprinkle the cakes with sugar and bake at 400° F. until pale brown.

Spice Cakes

Sift together

6 cups flour	2 cups dark molasses
$\frac{1}{2}$ tsp. allspice	2 cups sugar
1 tsp. cinnamon	3 tsp. soda
1 nutmeg grated	1 tbsp. dried orange peel
$\frac{1}{2}$ tsp. cloves	grated

Mix the sugar, molasses and orange peel together and bring it to a boil slowly. Add the soda and mix well. Add the hot foaming syrup to the flour and mix into a smooth dough. Knead thirty minutes. Roll to one-inch thickness, cut into small round cakes and bake at 350° F. for about twenty minutes.

Chocolate Cookies

Sift together

2$\frac{1}{2}$ cups flour	$\frac{1}{2}$ cup butter
$\frac{1}{4}$ tsp. salt	1 tbsp. lard
1 tsp. cinnamon	1 cup sugar
	1 egg unbeaten
Dissolve in	2 squares chocolate melted
2 tbsp. cold coffee	
$\frac{1}{2}$ tsp. soda	

Cream the butter, lard and sugar together until light. Add the chocolate and the egg and blend in thoroughly. Add the flour and coffee alternately. Have the dough as soft as it can be handled. Roll thin, cut into small cakes and bake at 400° F. six to eight minutes.

Fruit Snaps

Sift together

4 cups flour	1 cup butter
½ tsp. allspice	1½ cups brown sugar
2 tsp. cinnamon	1½ cups molasses

Mix

½ of the flour
2 cups currants
1 cup seeded raisins

Dissolve in

2 tbsp. milk
1 tsp. soda

Cream the butter and sugar together and add the molasses. Add the first half of the flour and mix well. Add the fruit mixture and milk alternately. Knead to a smooth dough. Roll thin, cut into small cakes and bake at 400° F. until brown.

Black Walnut Cakes

Black walnuts are without equal for cakes, in the opinion of some New England housewives. They are distinctive in flavor and unusual enough to be rated an excellency in food.

Sift together

3 cups flour	1 cup butter
½ tsp. soda	1½ cups sugar
1 tsp. cream of tartar	1 cup milk
½ tsp. salt	3 eggs unbeaten
	1 cup black walnut meats

Cream the butter and sugar together. Add the eggs and mix well. Add the flour and milk alternately. When all

of the flour is added mix in the nuts lightly. Roll the
dough to one-fourth inch thickness, cut into small squares
and bake at 450° F. until slightly brown. Reduce the
temperature to 350° F. and finish baking.

Hot Syrup Sponge Cake

Sponge cakes are favorite cakes the world over, and have
been for many generations. Hot syrup sponge cakes are
ancient in their origin. They were baked both as loaf
cakes and as small cakes long before the evolution of Modern American cookery.

4 cups cake flour sifted five times	8 egg whites beaten stiff
	8 egg yolks well beaten
2 cups sugar sifted three times	1 cup hot water
	$\frac{1}{4}$ tsp. almond extract

Boil the sugar and water together until the syrup spins
a thread. Fold the egg whites into the yolks. Gradually
add the hot syrup and continue beating until the mixture
is cold. Gradually fold in the flour and add the almond
extract. Fill small buttered moulds three-fourths full and
bake at 325° F. for eighteen to twenty minutes.

SCOTCH COOKIES IN COLONIAL AMERICA

Oatmeal cookies originated in Scotland, it is said. A surprising number of these cake recipes can be found in America. And many housewives will tell you they are very very old. Oatmeal cookies are more common now in New England than they are in the South but there was such an interchange of recipes between housewives in New England and their relatives and friends in the Southern states that it is difficult to determine just when some of the famous Scotch recipes found their home in America. The exchange of recipes brought to light interesting stories of how the families came by their cherished formulas for cake baking. For example, the Scotch Bread recipe used in the author's family was sent by a thoughtful Rhode Island housewife to her young kinsman, John Perry, who had married and moved to North Carolina. The recipe came to her through another young kinsman who had been "home" to England and returned to the New World with a Scotch wife.

Scotch Queen Cakes

Sift together

½ lb. powdered sugar
1½ tsp. cinnamon
½ tsp. mace

1 cup butter melted and
  cooled
4 cups rolled oats
½ lb. currants

Roll the rolled oats with a rolling pin until very fine. Add the sugar and mix well. Work in the butter, adding a little water if needed to make a stiff dough. Work in the currants. Roll the dough into a round sheet one inch thick. Cut into fourths, prick with a fork and scallop the edges. Bake at 400° F. until light brown.

Culpepper Oatmeal Cakes

Sift together

2 cups flour
½ tsp. salt

Dissolve in

1 tbsp. hot water
1 tsp. soda

2 cups rolled oats
1 cup sugar
⅓ cup butter
⅔ cup lard
2 tbsp. milk
2 egg yolks unbeaten
2 egg whites beaten stiff
1 lb. raisins
1 tsp. vanilla

Cream the butter, lard and sugar together. Add the egg yolks and blend well. Add the milk, vanilla and soda and stir until creamy. Add the raisins and fold in the egg whites. Add the flour and rolled oats and mix quickly and lightly. Drop into small cakes and bake at 450° F. for about ten minutes.

"Oat Cakes"

This recipe and the one just preceding came from the same New Hampshire housewife. "That is just an *oat cake* recipe," she said, "that I like specially, because grandmother always made them for us when we went to the farm to visit at Thanksgiving. We ate them warm, and no cake has ever tasted as good since."

Sift together

2 cups flour	1 cup lard
1 tsp. soda	2 cups sugar
1 tsp. cloves	1 cup sour milk
1 tsp. cinnamon	2 eggs unbeaten
1 tsp. ginger	

Mix with

2 cups oatmeal

Cream the sugar and lard together. Add the eggs, one at a time, and mix well. Add the milk and flour alternately and blend into a smooth batter. Fill small, well greased moulds half full and bake at 400° F. for about twenty minutes.

Sorghum Cakes

This is one of the author's old family recipes that came to Virginia from Scotland long before the Revolution, and was as much a part of the family traditions as the clan spirit of loyalty to kinsmen.

10 cups flour sifted	2 cups butter
2 cups sugar	2 cups of sorghum
1 tsp. soda	1 tbsp. vinegar

Blend the butter into the flour until the mixture is mealy. Boil the sugar and molasses together. Remove from the fire, add the soda and vinegar, and stir until it foams. Pour the hot mixture into the flour and knead into a smooth dough. Roll medium thin, cut into small squares and bake at 400° F. until light brown. These cakes keep well.

Arrowroot Cakes

No list of Scotch cake recipes would be complete without arrowroot cakes. This is an old recipe, considered choice by both New England and Southern housewives.

Sift together

1 lb. arrowroot flour	1 cup butter softened
½ cup powdered sugar	6 egg whites beaten stiff
	½ tsp. almond extract

Beat the butter until white and creamy. Add the almond extract. Gradually add the arrowroot. Fold in the egg whites and beat with a flat wire whip for twenty minutes. Spread the batter one inch thick in well buttered baking pans and bake at 350° F. for thirty minutes. Allow to cool before removing the cakes from the pans. Cut into small squares and sprinkle with sugar.

Scotch Short Bread

This is real Scotch short bread. The usual American recipe calls for too much sugar.

Sift together

¾ lb. flour (3 cups)	1 cup butter medium soft
½ lb. rice flour	6 tbsp. sugar

Add the flour and sugar alternately to the butter and knead to a smooth dough. Shape into medium thick round cakes the size of a saucer, prick with a fork and flute the edges. Bake at 400° F. about thirty minutes.

DUTCH RECIPES IN NEW YORK AND PENNSYLVANIA

The old Dutch recipes of New York and Pennsylvania seemed to have been absorbed by the housewives of English origin. But occasionally one will be the recipient of a recipe from a Van Horne or a Van Buskirk, with the assurance that it is real old Dutch and one immediately goes to the kitchen to try it out just to see how different it really is from old English recipes. The cakes turn out to be so English one is reminded that New Amsterdam and New England very soon began that fusing of customs that was to make America.

Molasses Drop Cookies

Sift together

6 cups flour
½ tsp. salt
1 tsp. ginger

Dissolve in

1 cup hot water
1 tsp. soda

1 cup molasses
1 cup sugar
1 cup butter
3 eggs unbeaten

Cream the butter and sugar together. Add the eggs, one at a time, and mix well. Add the molasses and beat until light. Gradually add the flour. When the batter begins to get too stiff to stir, add the hot water, a little at a time. Drop into small cookies and bake at 400° F. for twelve to fifteen minutes.

43

Soft Sugar Cookies

This is another cookie recipe that is said to be very old Dutch.

Sift together

4 cups flour	2 eggs unbeaten
½ tsp. salt	1 cup lard
1 tsp. soda	2½ cups sugar
	1 cup buttermilk
	1 tsp. vanilla

Blend the lard into the flour. Be careful to keep the mixture cold. Mix in the sugar. Add the eggs, buttermilk and flavoring and mix quickly. Knead slightly. Roll medium thick, cut into large cookies and bake at 450° F. about twelve minutes.

Risen Doughnuts

This is a typical Pennsylvania and New York recipe. The American doughnut of today came originally from Holland.

8 cups flour sifted	2 cups milk warmed
1 cup light brown sugar	1 yeast cake
1 cup butter	1 tsp. salt

Crumble the yeast into a bowl. Add one cup of milk. When the yeast begins to bubble add the flour, salt, sugar and the rest of the milk. Mix into a smooth dough and knead until blisters can be seen on the surface of the dough. Set in a warm place to rise to twice the bulk. Then knead the butter into the dough, blending it in a little at a time. Shape into small thin cakes. Fry in boiling fat to a light brown. Drain on brown paper and sprinkle with powdered sugar.

RECIPES FROM NEW ORLEANS

America has one city that stands apart from its neighbors, New Orleans. New Orleans has managed to hold on to its glamour which is the very soul of it. One finds a little Tea Shop tucked away in a narrow thoroughfare, a *banquette*, of the French Quarter. One is so interested in the beautiful old iron grill-work adorning an overhanging balcony that tea is forgotten for a time. Then a sudden inspiration comes. It shan't be tea, after all, but coffee. Dark amber colored coffee made by the drip method is the beverage for the occasion. New Orleans' French Quarter has always been famous for drip coffee. It is sure to be excellent.

And little cakes to go with the coffee! It is delightful to find the same kind of little cakes one ate, as a child on that memorable first trip to New Orleans, when the city still had some open sewers, and some tiny shops where urchins purchased a "quartee red beans, a quartee rice, lagnappe salt pork to make it taste nice." That meant a half nickle's worth each of red beans and rice, and lagnappe was something for nothing, the little gift of salt pork.

Cocoanut Drop Cookies

Sift together

1 cup flour
1 tsp. baking powder

1 cup sugar
1 cocoanut shredded
½ cup butter
1 egg unbeaten

Cream the butter and sugar together. Add the egg and cocoanut and mix well. Add the flour, using more if the

45

mixture is too soft to drop into small cakes. Bake at 450° F. for ten to fifteen minutes.

Creole Cocoanut Macaroons

Sift together

1 cup sugar	$\frac{1}{3}$ lb. cocoanut
2 tsp. corn starch	3 egg whites beaten stiff
$\frac{1}{8}$ tsp. salt	1 tsp. vanilla

Gradually add the sugar to the eggs, beating all the time. When all is added, stir in the cocoanut and vanilla. Bake the same as Cocoanut Drop Cookies.

French Fruit Cookies

Sift together

5 cups flour	2 cups brown sugar
$\frac{1}{4}$ tsp. nutmeg	1 cup sour cream
1 tsp. cinnamon	$1\frac{1}{2}$ cups butter
1 tsp. mace	2 cups raisins chopped
	3 egg yolks well beaten
Dissolve in	3 egg whites beaten stiff
1 tbsp. hot water	
1 tsp. soda	

Cream the butter and sugar together. Add the egg yolks and fold in the egg whites. Add the cream and then the soda. Stir in the flour and raisins and work into a smooth dough. Roll thin, cut into small cakes and bake at 350° F. for about twenty minutes.

Clabber Cake

Clabber is a favorite food in New Orleans. Milk is set in a cool place to coagulate from lactic acid bacteria in the air. It is eaten just as clabber or the cream is skimmed off and the coagulated milk is put into colander-like molds and allowed to drip over night. The curd is served with thick sour cream and sugar.

Clabber is much used in cookery. The whey is poured off and the thick sour milk is used, with excellent results.

Sift together

2 cups flour	1 cup sugar
2 tbsp. cocoa	1 cup clabber
1 tsp. soda	½ cup butter
½ tsp. salt	1 egg well beaten

Cream the butter and sugar together, add the egg, then the clabber and beat vigorously. Gradually add the flour. Spread the batter one-half inch thick in a well buttered baking pan and bake at 350° F. for about twenty minutes. Cut into small squares and ice with Mocha Icing.

To make mocha icing:

1 cup unsalted butter well creamed	2 tbsp. sugar
2 egg yolks slightly beaten	very strong coffee infusion

Beat the egg yolks into the butter. Add the sugar gradually and the coffee, a few drops at a time. Spread the cakes. Allow them to stand in the refrigerator twenty-four hours before serving.

Pecan Cakes

Sift together

2 cups flour	1 cup butter
½ cup powdered sugar	1 tsp. vanilla

Mix with

1½ cups ground pecans

Break the butter into small pieces and add it to the flour. Add the vanilla. Blend with the hands to a smooth dough. Form into crescent shaped cakes. Bake at 350° F. until light brown.

Cocoanut Pralines

The traveler in New Orleans has a *praline* to finish his afternoon coffee. The New Orleans housewife has borrowed the French word *praline* and used it to name her own confection which is a candy, not a cake.

1 cocoanut grated	1 cup sugar
½ cup water	

Cook the sugar and water together in a granite pot until the syrup begins to crystalize around the edges. Scrape the sides of the pot until free from sugar, add the cocoanut and cook until the mixture boils vigorously. Drop from a dessert spoon onto a marble slab.

MODERN AMERICAN RECIPES

Many of the typical Modern American recipes for cookies are very much like the old formulas. The vast step forward in American culinary art is not so much a definite change in the kinds of foods prepared as in the methods of preparation.

The American woman has discarded slow, meticulous methods brought from the Old World. She has discovered easy, quick methods to take their place.

The author had an excellent opportunity to compare present day American woman's methods of cooking with those that are still used by her neighbors in Europe.

The opportunity came through observing a cooking class for housewives, in one of the world famous Homemaking Schools in Sweden. Twelve young women were making cookies. One of those young women was busy with a task that seemed endless. She was cutting blanched almonds with a paring knife. She was shaving the almonds as fine as the American woman could do it in her cheap little nut grinder. She was spending several hours doing a job that the American woman would finish in fifteen minutes.

The American woman is not satisfied to accept a quick, easy way unless it is just as efficacious as the old method. She grinds the nuts with a cheap little nut grinder and to keep them from being oily she has discovered that they must be thoroughly chilled before and after grinding. Her ingenuity has been the means of evolving Modern American recipes that are typically her own. They employ Modern American methods which meet the needs of the woman who wants independence and knows it can never be achieved without leisure to follow her own personal inclinations.

Queens Gingerbread

Mix

6 cups flour sifted
½ lb. candied orange peel
   sliced thin

Sift together

6 cups flour
½ tsp. nutmeg
½ tsp. cloves
½ tsp. mace

2 lbs. honey
1¾ lbs. brown sugar
½ cup water
1½ lbs. almonds blanched
   and sliced thin

Heat the honey, sugar and water together slowly until it boils. Add the almonds and remove from the fire. Add the flour and spices, then the flour and orange peel. Put the dough in the refrigerator for twenty-four hours. Form into little balls with the hands and bake at 400° F. until light brown.

While the cakes are still hot brush them lightly with a syrup made of 1 cup of sugar and ⅓ cup of water. Cook the syrup to the soft ball stage.

Overnight Gingerbread

Sift together

4 cups flour
½ tsp. salt
1 tsp. soda
2 tbsp. Jamaica ginger

1 cup sugar
1 cup butter
½ cup light molasses
2 eggs unbeaten

Cream the butter and sugar together.   Add the eggs, one at a time, and mix well.   Add the molasses and flour alternately.   Knead into a smooth dough.   Shape into two rolls and place in the refrigerator over night.   Slice thin and bake at 400° F. until light brown.

This dough will keep in the refrigerator for a week or more.

Butterscotch Cakes

Sift together

7 cups flour	1 cup butter
1 tsp. soda	4 eggs well beaten
1 tsp. salt	
1 tsp. cream of tartar	

Mix with

4 cups brown sugar

Blend the butter into the flour until the mixture is mealy. Add the eggs and knead into a smooth dough.   Shape the dough into two rolls and place in the refrigerator over night.   Bake as directed for Overnight Gingerbread.

This dough will keep a week in the refrigerator if it is put away in a closely covered container.

Butterscotch Cookies

Butterscotch seems a favorite name to apply to cookies made with brown sugar.   This cake is especially good in spite of its *stock name*.

Sift together

5½ cups flour	2½ cups brown sugar
1 tsp. soda	2 cups molasses
	¾ cup butter
	1 cocoanut grated

Cream the butter and sugar together. Add the molasses, flour and cocoanut alternately. Knead into a stiff dough, adding more flour if needed. Let stand over night in the refrigerator. Shape into little balls and bake at 400° F. for ten to fifteen minutes. Let the cookies cool before removing them from the pans.

Butter Cookies

Here is an ice box cookie that is certainly the old dressed up all new. Just butter, eggs, sugar and flour. No flavoring. The typical old recipe. Yet it is modern, a splendid example of our American cookery.

4 cups flour sifted
1 cup sugar

2 cups butter softened slightly
2 eggs beaten slightly

Break the butter in large pieces. Add the sugar and the eggs and blend with a pastry blender until creamy. Add the flour gradually, blending it in with the pastry blender. Mold the dough into seven little rolls and put in the ice box until firm. Shape into long cookies with a cookie press and bake at 400° F. until light brown.

American Short Bread

Liberties were taken with Scotch Short Bread in formulating this recipe.

8 cups flour sifted
2 cups butter creamed
1 tbsp. caraway seed

1¾ cups sugar
6 eggs unbeaten

Add the sugar, eggs and caraway seed to the butter and mix well. Blend in the flour and knead into a smooth dough. Roll one-fourth inch thick, cut into small squares, mark the cakes with a cross, using the back of a knife, and bake at 400° F. for about fifteen minutes.

Brown Sugar Short Bread

Here is a typical modern American Scotch Short Bread recipe. It was formulated and used frequently by a Scotch-American housewife.

2 cups flour sifted
½ cup butter

½ cup light brown sugar
1 egg unbeaten

Cream the butter and sugar until light. Add the egg and mix well. Blend in the flour and knead the dough until smooth. Roll medium thin and cut into squares. Bake at 400° F. until light brown.

Card Gingerbread

Sift together

8 cups flour
1 tsp. ginger
1 tsp. salt

1 cup lard
1 cup sugar
1 cup molasses

Dissolve in

½ cup water
1 tsp. soda

Cream the sugar and lard together. Add the molasses and mix well. Add the flour and water alternately and mix into a soft dough. Roll thin and cut into squares with a knife. Bake at 400° F. until light brown.

Orange Wafers

To the European woman a wafer is a delicate, paper-thin cake cooked in a wafer iron. The American housewife calls any very thin small cake a wafer. This is a delicate and delicious tea cake, an excellent example of wafers.

3 cups flour sifted	4 egg yolks slightly beaten
1 cup sugar	2 tsp. orange juice
1 cup butter	1 tsp. orange extract

Cream the butter and sugar together. Gradually add the orange juice and the orange extract. Begin blending in the flour and egg yolks working the dough as little as possible. Roll very thin and cut into small round cakes. Bake at 400° F. until light brown.

Vanilla Wafers

Sift together

3 cups flour	½ cup lard
2 tsp. baking powder	1½ cups sugar
½ tsp. salt	2 tbsp. milk
	2 eggs unbeaten
	1 tsp. vanilla

Cream the sugar and lard together. Add the eggs and vanilla and mix well. Add the flour and milk alternately. Knead to a smooth dough, roll very thin, cut into small round cakes and bake at 400° F. until light brown.

Peanut Wafers

Sift together

1 cup flour	1 egg unbeaten
½ tsp. soda	1 cup sugar
Mix with	2 tbsp. butter softened
	2 tbsp. milk

1 cup roasted peanuts
chopped
½ tsp. salt

Mix the sugar, butter, milk and egg together and blend thoroughly. Add the flour and nuts and stir up quickly. Drop into small cakes and bake at 400° F. until light brown. Reduce the temperature and finish baking.

These wafers spread to a thin cake and are crisp when baked properly.

Walnut Wafers

Sift together

3 heaping tbsp. flour	1 cup brown sugar
⅛ tsp. salt	2 eggs beaten ten minutes

Mix with

1 cup walnuts chopped

Add the sugar to the eggs and beat three minutes. Fold in the flour. Drop into small cakes and bake at 400° F. for about five minutes. These are a very thin crisp wafer.

Oatmeal Wafers

Mix

	1 tsp. vanilla
2½ cups rolled oats	1 cup sugar
2 tsp. baking powder	1 tbsp. butter melted
½ tsp. salt	2 eggs beaten ten minutes

Gradually add the sugar to the eggs. Add the butter and vanilla and stir in the oatmeal. Drop into small cakes and bake at 400° F. eight to ten minutes.

Almond Wafers

½ cup almonds blanched
and ground
½ lb. powdered sugar sifted

1 tbsp. milk
4 egg whites beaten stiff

Gradually add the milk to the almonds, blending the mixture into a paste. Add the sugar gradually. After all the sugar is added thin with milk until it will run off the spoon. Fold in the egg whites. Bake in a wafer iron and roll while hot.

Cocoanut Wafers

4 cups flour sifted

Dissolve in

1 tbsp. hot water
½ tsp. soda

2 cups sugar
½ cup butter
1 cup sour milk
2 tsp. rose water
1 small cocoanut grated
5 egg yolks well beaten
5 egg whites beaten stiff

Cream the butter and sugar together. Work in the ingredients in the following order: the egg yolks, then the flour and milk alternately, the soda, rose water, cocoanut and the egg whites. Drop into small cakes and bake at 400° F. until light brown. Remove from the baking sheets at once. If allowed to cool they break.

Plain Jumbles

Jumbles are very old. *Jumbals* we find them in some of the oldest cook books. These jumbals were made into a stiff dough and formed into little rings with the hands.

3 cups flour sifted
1 cup sugar
2 tbsp. cream

½ cup butter creamed
4 eggs well beaten

Mix the butter, sugar and eggs together and beat until light. Add the flour and cream alternately and knead into a smooth dough. Form into little rings with the hands, brush with egg white, sprinkle with coarse sugar and cinnamon and bake at 400° F. until light brown.

Fried Jumbles

Sift together

6 cups flour	1 cup sugar
3 tsp. baking powder	$\frac{1}{2}$ cup butter
$\frac{1}{2}$ nutmeg grated	1 cup milk
$\frac{1}{2}$ tsp. salt	2 eggs unbeaten

Cream the butter and sugar together. Add the eggs, one at a time, and mix well. Add the flour and milk alternately and knead into a smooth dough. Form into little rings with the hands and cook in boiling fat until light brown.

Cinnamon Fruit Cookies

Fruit cookies are surprisingly alike be they English, French, Dutch or America. They are always a favorite and the American housewife prides herself on the fruit and nut mixtures she uses in small cake making.

Sift together

4 cups flour	1 cup butter softened
1 tsp. soda	2 cups sugar
1 tsp. cinnamon	$\frac{1}{2}$ cup milk
$\frac{1}{2}$ tsp. nutmeg	2 eggs unbeaten
$\frac{1}{4}$ tsp. cloves	
$\frac{1}{2}$ tsp. salt	

Mix with

1 cup raisins chopped

Mix the butter, sugar and eggs together and beat until light. Add the flour and milk alternately and knead into a soft dough. Roll to one-fourth inch thickness, cut into small cakes and bake at 400° F. for about fifteen minutes.

These cookies keep well and are a favorite Christmas cake.

Quick Filled Cookies

Sift together

3 cups flour	1 cup butter
1½ tsp. baking powder	1 cup sugar
	2 eggs unbeaten
	1 tbsp. cream

Cream the butter and sugar together. Add the eggs, one at a time, and mix well. Add the flour and cream and knead into a smooth dough. Roll thin, cut into small round cakes and bake at 400° F. until light brown. Fill the cakes with:

1 tbsp. butter creamed	½ cup candied orange peel
3 tbsp. heavy cream	chopped
1 cup powdered sugar	¼ cup nuts ground
sifted	
1 tsp. vanilla	

Gradually add the cream and vanilla to the butter. Add the sugar until the filling is of the consistency to spread. Add the orange peel and nuts. Spread the cakes and stick two together.

Filled Cookies

Sift together

3½ cups flour
3 tsp. baking powder
½ tsp. salt

1 cup sugar
½ cup butter
½ cup milk
2 eggs unbeaten
1 tsp. vanilla

Cream the butter and sugar together. Add the eggs and vanilla and mix well. Add the flour and milk alternately and knead into a smooth dough. Roll thin and cut into large round cakes. Fill with the following:

½ cup sugar
½ cup water
1 tbsp. flour

½ cup candied orange peel chopped
½ cup raisins chopped
¼ cup butter

Mix the flour, sugar and water together. Add the butter and raisins and cook until thick. Remove from the heat and add the orange peel. Place a small spoon of the filling in the center of each cake. Place another cake on top and press the edges together. Bake at 400° F. for about fifteen minutes.

Christmas Fruit Cookies

Sift together

3 cups flour
1 tsp. cinnamon
¼ tsp. nutmeg
1 tsp. soda

1 cup butter creamed
1 cup brown sugar
3 eggs unbeaten

Mix with

1 cup raisins chopped
½ cup currants
1 cup dates chopped
½ cup cocoanut

Mix the butter, sugar and eggs together and beat until light. Add the flour and stir into a stiff dough. Drop into small cakes and bake at 400° F. for about fifteen minutes.

Fruit Drop Cookies

This recipe is patterned after the oldest fruit biscuits of England. The prunes and baking powder are the modern innovation.

Sift together

4 cups flour
1 tsp. baking powder

1½ cups butter softened
1 cup brown sugar
2 eggs unbeaten

Mix with

1 cup seeded raisins
1 cup walnuts chopped
½ lb. citron chopped
1 cup prunes chopped
1 cocoanut grated

Dissolve in

1 tbsp. water
1 tsp. soda

Mix the butter, sugar and eggs together and beat until light. Add the flour and water and mix into a smooth dough. Roll one-eighth inch thick and cut into two-inch squares with a sharp knife. Brush the cakes with egg white and sprinkle them with:

Mix together

⅓ lb. almonds blanched
   and ground

1 cup sugar

Bake the cakes at 400° F. for about fifteen minutes.

Raisin Cookies

Sift together

2 cups flour
2 tsp. baking powder
¼ tsp. nutmeg

Mix with

1 cup raisins

2 tbsp. butter melted
1 cup sugar
2 eggs beaten ten minutes
1 tsp. vanilla

Gradually add the sugar to the eggs. Add the butter and vanilla and beat until light. Fold in the flour. Drop into small cakes and bake at 400° F. for twelve to fifteen minutes.

Hard Fruit and Nut Cakes

Sift together

3 cups flour
1 tsp. cinnamon
½ tsp. salt

Dissolve in

1 tbsp. hot water
1 tsp. soda

½ cup sugar
1 cup brown sugar
1 cup butter softened
3 eggs slightly beaten
1 lb. walnuts chopped
¾ lb. raisins chopped

Mix the sugar, butter and eggs together and mix well. Add the fruit and nuts. Stir in the flour and soda and mix just enough to blend in thoroughly. Drop into small cakes and bake at 400° F. for about fifteen minutes.

This cookie is a favorite with thrifty housewives because of its keeping qualities. They will keep for several months.

Date Drops

Sift together

1½ cups flour
1 tsp. baking powder
1 tsp. cinnamon
½ tsp. cloves
¼ tsp. salt

½ cup butter softened
1 cup sugar
2 eggs slightly beaten
1 cup pecans chopped

Dissolve in

4 tbsp. water
1 tsp. soda

Mix with

1 lb. dates chopped

Mix the sugar, butter and eggs together and beat until light. Add the dates and the nuts. Fold in the flour. Drop into small cakes and bake at 425° F. for eight to ten minutes.

These cakes keep well. Dates hold moisture in cookies and prevent them from drying out.

Date Strips

Sift together

1 cup flour
1 tsp. baking powder

3 egg whites beaten stiff
1 cup sugar

Mix with

1 cup chopped dates
1 cup chopped nuts

Fold the sugar into the egg whites. Add the flour, all at once and blend quickly but lightly. Turn into a well buttered pan nine by thirteen inches and bake at 350° F. for thirty minutes. Cut into narrow strips while warm and roll in powdered sugar.

Nut Cookies

Sift together

3 cups flour
¼ tsp. salt

Mix with

1 cup walnuts chopped

Dissolve in

2 tbsp. hot water
1 tsp. soda

2 cups brown sugar
1 cup butter
3 eggs unbeaten

Cream the butter and sugar together. Add the eggs, one at a time and beat until light. Add the flour and soda alternately. Drop into small cookies and bake at 425° F. for ten to fifteen minutes.

Walnut Cookies

Sift together

6 cups flour
1 tsp. salt
1 tsp. Jamaica ginger
1 tsp. soda

1 cup molasses
1 cup sugar
½ cup milk
¼ lb. walnuts chopped
coarse sugar

Mix the molasses, sugar and milk together and stir until the sugar is dissolved. Add the liquid gradually to the flour and knead into a smooth dough. Roll very thin, cut into two-inch squares, brush with milk and sprinkle with sugar and nuts. Bake at 400° F. until light brown.

Chocolate Pecan Cookies

Sift together

4 cups flour
1 tsp. soda

1 lb. light brown sugar
1 cup butter softened
2 squares chocolate grated
1 cup milk
2 eggs slightly beaten
¼ lb. pecans chopped

Cook the milk and chocolate together until thick and smooth. Allow to cool and add the nuts. Blend the butter, sugar and eggs together until light. Add the chocolate and fold in the flour, mixing as little as possible. Drop into small cakes and bake at 425° F. until light brown.

Plain Meringues

Meringues are easily made. American housewives like their meringues "chewy." If they are made the *easy way,* with little beating, and baked at 250° F. to 275° F. for about thirty minutes they will be "chewy." The real success of good meringues depends upon two things: fresh eggs and sufficient beating of the egg whites before any sugar is added.

2 egg whites beaten dry   1 cup sugar sifted
¼ tsp. pure vanilla

Gradually add the sugar to the egg whites, beating all the time. Add the vanilla with the last sugar. Drop into small cakes and bake at 250° F. for thirty minutes.

Grease the baking pans with butter. Remove the meringues while hot. Recipe makes six meringues to serve as a base for ice cream, etc.

Nut Meringues

2 egg whites beaten stiff
½ cup sugar sifted

⅛ tsp. salt
¼ tsp. vanilla
½ cup nuts chopped fine

Gradually add the sugar to the egg whites, beating all the time. Add the vanilla, salt and chopped nuts. Drop into small cakes and bake at 275° F. for twenty minutes. This recipe makes twenty small meringues.

Date and Nut Meringues

3 egg whites beaten stiff
¾ cup sugar sifted
¾ cup unblanched almonds
  chopped
¾ cup dates chopped

⅛ tsp. salt
¼ tsp. almond extract

Gradually add the sugar to the egg whites, beating all the time. Add the almond extract, salt, nuts and dates and fold in lightly. Drop into small cakes and bake at 275° F. for about twenty minutes.

Cinnamon Nut Meringues

4 egg whites beaten stiff
1 cup sugar

½ lb. almonds blanched
  and chopped
1⅛ tsp. cinnamon

Gradually add the sugar to the egg whites. Add the cinnamon and fold in the nuts. Drop into small cakes and bake at 275° F. for about thirty minutes.

Almond Macaroons

1 lb. powdered sugar sifted
4 egg whites unbeaten
$\frac{3}{4}$ lb. almonds blanched
  and shredded

$\frac{1}{2}$ tsp. cinnamon
1 tsp. vanilla

Gradually add the sugar to the egg whites and beat for thirty minutes. Add the almonds and flavoring. Bake as directed for Cinnamon Nut Meringues.

Peanut Macaroons

$\frac{1}{2}$ lb. roasted peanuts unblanched, ground
  through the food chop-
  per
$\frac{1}{2}$ lb. powdered sugar sifted

$\frac{1}{2}$ tbsp. flour sifted
$\frac{1}{8}$ tsp. salt
$\frac{1}{2}$ tsp. vanilla
1 egg beaten ten minutes

Add the sugar to the egg and beat three minutes. Fold in the nuts, salt, flour and vanilla. Drop into small cakes and bake at 300° F. for twenty minutes.

Pecan Macaroons

1 cup brown sugar
1 cup pecans chopped

$\frac{1}{4}$ tsp. salt
1 egg white beaten stiff
$\frac{1}{4}$ tsp. lemon extract

Gradually add the sugar to the egg white. Add the salt and fold in the nuts lightly. Drop into small cakes and bake at 275° F. for about thirty minutes.

Cocoanut Macaroons

1 egg white beaten stiff
⅛ cup sweetened condensed milk

1½ cups cocoanut
½ tsp. vanilla

Mix the cocoanut and condensed milk together. Add the vanilla and fold in the egg white. Drop into small cakes and bake at 300° F. until light brown.

Cocoanut Meringues

4 egg whites beaten dry
½ lb. powdered sugar sifted

1 cup cocoanut or more
¼ tsp. lemon extract

Gradually add the sugar to the egg whites. Add the flavoring and stir in cocoanut until the mixture is stiff. Drop into small cakes and bake at 300° F. for about fifteen minutes.

Cocoanut Balls

These are very much like the old-fashioned cocoanut biscuits which Virginia housewives take such pride in making. They are more like a candy than a cake, but to the person who thinks there is nothing more delectable than the taste of cocoanut they are a welcomed cake for Afternoon Tea.

1 lb. cocoanut
2 egg whites unbeaten

2 cups sugar

Mix the ingredients together and cook rapidly, stirring constantly, for twelve minutes. Turn the mixture out on a marble slab or a metal topped table and allow to cool. Form into little balls and bake at 350° F. until light brown.

Lady Fingers

Little Sponge Cakes are not as popular with the modern housewife as they should be. For some unknown reason she has the notion they are hard to make. There is nothing mysterious about sponge cake making. Try this recipe and prove it.

Sift together three times
$\frac{1}{3}$ cup cake flour
$\frac{1}{2}$ tsp. salt

$\frac{1}{2}$ tsp. vanilla
$\frac{1}{2}$ cup powdered sugar sifted
2 egg yolks beaten ten minutes
2 egg whites beaten stiff

Add the sugar to the egg yolks. Fold in the flour and then the egg whites and the vanilla. Shape into lady fingers by using a pastry bag and tube. Bake at 325° F. for eighteen to twenty minutes.

COOKIES MADE WITH WINE

THE modern American housewife knows the value of wine in cake making. She is aware too that the alcoholic content is expelled by the heat of baking and there is left only the rich, full flavored quality characteristic of the liquors used.

Sweet wines are the cooking wines. They are known as *fortified wines*. The alcoholic content of this type of wine is increased by the addition of grape brandy until it ranges from twenty to twenty-two per cent. These are heavy, strong wines, more highly flavored, and more syrupy in character than the lighter kinds.

Sherry was originally a Spanish wine. It is the most prized of all the cooking wines. It retains its flavor better than any other sweet wine.

Port, Sherry, Muscatel, Tokay and Angelica are sweet wines of high grade that are being produced in America. Any of these American wines may be substituted in a recipe calling for Sherry.

Cocoanut Torte

Sift together

1½ cups flour
½ tsp. salt

½ cup butter
¼ cup brown sugar
2 tbsp. Sherry

Mix the flour, butter and sugar together and blend until crumbly. Add the wine, a few drops at a time, and mix in lightly. Press the pastry into a shallow baking pan eight by ten inches. Bake at 300° F. until the cake begins to set, then spread with the following:

Sift together

2 tbsp. flour
½ tsp. baking powder
⅛ tsp. salt

2 eggs beaten ten minutes

Mix with

1 cup cocoanut
1 cup nuts chopped
1½ cups brown sugar

Stir the eggs into the cocoanut mixture. Spread on the slightly baked crust and finish baking at 325° F. It takes about thirty minutes. Cool the cake slightly and ice with lemon icing.

Lemon Icing

1½ cups powdered sugar
    sifted
2 tbsp. lemon juice

1 tbsp. white wine (Moselle)

Gradually add the lemon juice and wine to the sugar. Beat until smooth and glossy. Let stand for five minutes before spreading it on the torte. Let the torte cool, then cut it into narrow strips.

Chocolate Torte

Sift together

1½ cups flour
¼ tsp. salt
¼ cup sugar

½ cup butter
1 egg yolk well beaten
1 tbsp. Sherry

Blend the butter into the flour. Gradually add the egg yolk and wine and mix into a crumbly dough. Press the dough into a pan eight by eight inches. Spread with a heavy plum jam and bake at 300° F. for eight minutes. Then spread with the following mixture:

4 egg yolks unbeaten
4 egg whites beaten stiff
1 cup sugar

1 cup sweet chocolate grated
2 tbsp. Sherry

Cream the egg yolks and sugar together for fifteen minutes. Add the chocolate and Sherry and fold in the egg whites. Spread on the partially cooked cake and bake at 325° F. for about thirty minutes. Allow to cool slightly and cut into small squares.

Date Torte

Sift together

2 cups flour
½ tsp. soda
½ tsp. salt

1 cup butter softened

Mix with

2 cups oatmeal (quick cooking kind)
2 cups brown sugar

Blend the butter into the flour mixture. Divide the dough into halves. Press one part into a shallow pan, about eight by ten inches. Spread with the following filling:

1 lb. dates chopped
1 cup brown sugar
1 cup Sherry
¼ tsp. nutmeg
¼ tsp. salt
dash black pepper

1 cup almonds blanched, browned in the oven, cooled and then chopped

Cook the dates, sugar, wine, salt, nutmeg and pepper together until thick. Cool slightly and add the nuts. Spread the mixture on the dough in the pan.

Have a sheet of wax paper the size of the pan on which to press the rest of the dough. The sheet of paper can then be lifted and laid dough side to the cake. Press down firmly and remove the paper. Smooth the dough evenly around the edges to keep the filling from boiling out. Bake at 350° F. for thirty minutes. Cool slightly and cut into small squares.

Orange Torte

Sift together

1¼ cups flour
½ cup sugar
1 tsp. baking powder
¼ tsp. salt
⅛ tsp. nutmeg

½ cup butter
3 tbsp. Sherry
3 egg yolks well beaten

Blend the butter into the flour until the mixture is mealy. Gradually add the egg yolks and wine. Spread thinly on a baking pan and sprinkle with:

Mix together

⅓ cup sugar
1 tsp. cinnamon
¼ cup pecans chopped
¼ cup candied orange peel
   chopped

After the mixture is evenly sprinkled on the cake press down with a broad bladed spatula so the nuts and orange peel will bake into the torte. Bake at 350° F. for about thirty minutes. Cut into small squares when cold.

Black Walnut Torte

Sift together

1⅔ cups flour
⅔ cup sugar
¼ tsp. salt
¼ tsp. nutmeg

½ cup butter
1 egg slightly beaten
2 tbsp. Sherry

Blend the butter into the flour mixture. Gradually add the egg and wine and knead into a smooth dough. Roll thin and line a shallow baking pan to a depth of about one inch. Bake until slightly set at 450° F. Spread with the following mixture:

⅔ cup sugar
½ cup black walnuts chopped
¼ cup citron cut fine
½ cup butter
⅛ tsp. salt
¼ tsp. almond extract
2 tbsp. Sherry

4 egg yolks unbeaten

Cream the butter, sugar and egg yolks together for fifteen minutes. Add the wine, almond extract, salt and nuts. Sprinkle the citron over the partially baked cake. Spread the filling on top and bake at 325° F. for about thirty minutes. Cut into small squares while warm and allow to cool in the pan before removing the cakes.

PART II

Cookies from Other Lands

CONTENTS

COOKIES FROM OTHER COUNTRIES

Cookies, as the American housewife knows them, are much alike in England, Scotland, Ireland, the Scandinavian Countries, and the Germanic Countries.

The American traveler looks about in other lands to find "Sweets" to supply the sugar he is in the habit of eating, and feels he must have, for the American consumes more sugar than the inhabitant of any other country. He can always find some sort of "Sweets" in whatever land he visits. They may not be entirely to his liking but they suffice, and frequently they are different enough to be interesting. He may be offered a strange nut paste in Turkey, a rich fried cake in Spain, or he may even have to stoop to chewing pieces of peeled sugar cane if he happens to be in an island of the Pacific which is unfrequented by world travelers. But he must not expect to find cookies as he knows them unless he happens to stumble upon just the right nomad habitation in western Asia. If such a thing should be his good fortune he may find a woman baking cakes before the tent door, like Sarah of Bible times. The cakes will be made of whole wheat flour, salt and water, and baked on a griddle, as the women made and baked cakes for the Sons of Abraham. Or they may be a sweet cake, and if they are, tradition says they were brought into the land by the traders who wandered far into the regions of western Russia to trade with the Vikings. These cakes are so similar to some of the oldest Scandinavian recipes that the tradition must be based on facts.

FRENCH RECIPES

THE author recalls a walk along the banks of the river Loire an autumn afternoon. The group of friends walking together that afternoon had little to say to each other. It was one of those times when perfect weather enhanced the loveliness of the landscape and made talk seem a sacrilege. The setting sun made a golden path across the water. The first pale grey of dusk seemed to bring with it an added stillness.

That stillness was broken by the French woman in the party. "Come, drink chocolate with me," she invited.

It is always *chocolat*, if the service is typically French. The beverage is made of water instead of milk. Cocoa, sugar and water are boiled together to a thick, creamy paste. Then hot water and heavy cream are added and the drink is beaten until frothy.

The French lady served the delicious *chocolat* in small, squat royal blue cups, which one sees in Orleans and plans to buy, without fail. And with the steaming hot drink, meringues were served. But they were not like American meringues. They were filled with whipped cream.

Meringues à la Crème

(Cream Meringues)

1 cup sugar   ¼ cup water
2 egg whites unbeaten

Mix the ingredients together in a granite saucepan. Set the pan in a pot of simmering water and stir constantly until the mixture is heavy enough to hold its shape. Remove the pan from the hot water and set it in cold water. Continue stirring until cool. Drop into small cookies and bake at 250° F. for forty-five minutes. Carefully crush in the bottoms of the meringues and allow them to cool. When ready to serve, fill the centers with whipped cream and press two meringues together.

Chaux au Chocolat

(Chocolate Cream Puffs)

1 cup flour sifted	2 tbsp. sugar
1 cup water	4 eggs unbeaten
⅓ cup butter	¼ tsp. salt

Heat the butter, sugar, salt and water together until it boils. Gradually add the flour and cook until the mixture does not stick to the pan. Stir constantly. Remove from the fire and add the eggs, one at a time. Mix well. Drop into small cakes and bake at 450° F. for twenty minutes. Reduce the heat to 325° F. and continue baking twenty minutes. Make a slit in the side of the cakes and fill with whipped cream. Ice the tops with sweet chocolate melted over hot water.

Vol-au-Vent, Chantilly

(Tarts)

Puff paste	sugar
egg slightly beaten	jam or marmalade

Roll puff paste thin. Cut with a fluted cutter. From half of the biscuits cut a ring from the center. Brush the biscuits with egg. Place one with a hole upon a whole biscuit. Bake at 450° F. for fifteen minutes. Just before removing the cakes from the oven sprinkle them with sugar and bake until glazed. Fill the centers with jam just before serving.

Gâteaux au Noix

(Walnut Cake)

4 egg whites well beaten	1 cup walnuts chopped
4 egg yolks well beaten	1 cup dry bread crumbs
grated rind of ½ lemon	⅛ tsp. mace
½ cup sugar	⅛ tsp. cloves

Blend the egg yolks and sugar together. Add the bread crumbs, nuts and flavoring. Fold in the egg whites. Spread thinly into a well buttered pan and bake at 350° F. for thirty minutes. Cut into small squares and spread with whipped cream just before serving.

Gâteaux Chambord

(Sponge Cake)

½ cup cake flour sifted three times	5 egg yolks unbeaten
½ cup sugar sifted	5 egg whites beaten stiff
½ tsp. salt	
1 tsp. vanilla	

Add the sugar, salt and vanilla to the egg yolks and beat ten minutes. Fold in the egg whites. Then lightly fold in the flour. Pour into a shallow baking pan and bake at 325° F. for thirty minutes. Cut into small squares when cold and spread with the following:

2 egg yolks unbeaten
2 tbsp. sugar
1 tbsp. flour
½ tsp. vanilla

1 cup milk
½ cup almonds blanched
   and chopped

Mix the egg yolks, sugar, flour and milk together in a double boiler and cook for five minutes. Stir to keep from lumping. Remove from the fire and add the almonds and vanilla. Cool before spreading the cakes.

Baba au Medére

(Madeira Bread)

Sift together

2½ cups flour
½ tsp. salt

Mix with

1 cup Sultana raisins

1½ cups flour sifted
1 cake compressed yeast
½ cup butter melted
1 cup milk warmed
½ cup milk cold
3 eggs well beaten

Break the yeast in small pieces and add it to the warm milk. When it begins to foam beat in the flour. Continue beating for five minutes. Let the batter rise in a warm place for two hours. Add the sponge, eggs, cold milk, and butter to the flour and raisins and mix into a smooth dough. Knead for ten minutes. Form into a thin cake, place in a well-greased pan, set in a warm place and let rise to twice the bulk. Bake at 375° F. for about thirty minutes.

Make a heavy syrup of 1 cup of sugar and 1 cup of water. When the syrup spins a thread remove from the fire and stir in 6 tablespoons of Madeira. Baste the warm cake with the syrup, putting on so little at a time that it does not soak into the cake. Cut in small squares when cold.

RECIPES FROM ITALY

ITALY is the land of enchantment. The traveler is so engaged with the feeling that he can never exhaust the charms of such cities as Naples and Venice, that he can never tire of the wonders of all the art treasures, and the historic interest of all the cathedrals, that for many days he is utterly unconscious of the food he eats.

Then one morning he awakens after a dinner the evening before with friends, and if he is an American he longs for the simple food of his homeland.

It was after just such an experience that the author looked about for a salad made of fresh vegetables and a simple "sweet."

The Italians eat very little sugar, in comparison with Northern Europeans, English and Americans. One must not expect to find many little cakes. But the author did find several.

Cavalucci di Italia

(Nut Cakes of Italy)

2 cups flour sifted
1 cup brown sugar
1 cup walnuts chopped
⅓ cup candied orange peel chopped
⅛ tsp. each: nutmeg, cinnamon, cloves
½ tsp. anise seed

½ cup hot water

Cook the sugar and water together until the syrup spins a thread. Remove from the fire and add the nuts, spices and orange peel. Add the flour and knead into a smooth dough. Roll thin, cut into small cakes and bake at 350° F. until light brown.

Colombos

(Doves)

2 cups flour sifted	2 tbsp. cream
½ cup butter	2 egg yolks unbeaten
½ cup sugar	

Cream the butter and sugar together. Add the egg yolks and blend in well. Add the flour and enough cream to make a stiff dough. Roll thin, cut with a cutter shaped like a bird, mark eyes with currants and bake at 350° F. to a golden brown.

Dolce Ravioli

(Fried Tarts)

Sift together

1½ cups flour	3 tbsp. butter
½ tsp. salt	¼ cup water or less

Blend the butter into the flour. Add enough water to make a stiff dough. Roll very thin and cut into small squares. Make tarts with the following filling:

½ lb. cottage cheese	2 egg yolks unbeaten
2 tbsp. sugar	¼ tsp. vanilla

Mix the ingredients together and rub through a sieve. Place a teaspoon of the mixture in the center of a square of pastry.   Place another square on top.   Press the edges securely together and fry in hot olive oil until light brown. Drain and sprinkle with sugar.

Pan Dolci

(Fruit Bread)

Sift together

6 cups flour	1 cake compressed yeast
2 tsp. salt	warm water as needed

Break the yeast into one cup of warm water and let stand until it begins to foam.   Make a sponge of the flour, yeast and enough warm water to make a thick batter.   Beat it until it begins to bubble.   Let rise in a warm place for several hours.   Then add:

2 cups butter melted	¼ cup pistachio nuts
2 cups sugar	½ cup citron chopped
1 cup pine nuts	3 tbsp. Sherry
1 cup Sultana raisins	2 tbsp. orange flower water
½ cup seeded raisins	flour to make a dough
½ cup currants	

When all the ingredients are added blend in flour to make a smooth dough.   Knead for ten minutes.   Let rise to twice the bulk.   Shape into loaves and let rise to twice the bulk.   Bake at 400° F. for one hour or more.   Cut into strips and toast before serving.

RECIPES FROM SPAIN

THE traveler remembers Spain of the past. Romantic Spain, with its tropical flowers, its beautiful women, its suave mannered men, its cities permeated with Moorish influence of olden times, its historic cathedrals, makes a pleasant spot in memory that is cherished, for never again will the traveler see Spain as it was in the past.

He will remember, too, with a little thrill of pleasure, having breakfast in bed, a late breakfast of chocolate and a queer sort of fritter called *churos,* the national meal of all Spaniards.

Churos

(Fritters)

1¼ cups flour sifted
¼ cup butter
1 cup water
1 tbsp. Sherry
3 eggs slightly beaten

Heat the water and butter together to the boiling point. Remove from the fire and gradually add the flour. Then cook, stirring constantly, until the paste no longer adheres to the spoon. Again remove from the fire. Add the eggs and wine gradually, blending them in thoroughly. Put the paste in a pastry bag. Use a small tube and squeeze the dough into hot oil, in lengths of ten to twelve inches. As the paste touches the hot fat it curls into round fritters. Fry to a golden brown. Drain and sprinkle with sugar.

Biscochos

(Biscuit)

3 cups flour sifted $\frac{1}{2}$ cup butter softened
1 tbsp. grated orange peel   6 egg yolks unbeaten
1 tbsp. Sherry

Mix the butter, egg yolks, orange peel and wine together and beat well. Gradually add the flour and knead to a smooth dough. Mold into *twists* and brush with egg. Bake at 375° F. until golden brown.

Ojaldas

(Fried Cakes)

Sift together

1 cup flour   2 eggs well beaten
$\frac{1}{4}$ tsp. salt

Blend the flour into the eggs. Knead ten minutes, adding more flour if needed to make a stiff dough. Let the dough stand one hour. Roll very thin, cut into diamond shapes and fry in hot oil. Drain and sprinkle with powdered sugar.

ENGLISH CAKES

WHEREVER one goes in England, be it tavern or cottage, manor house or castle, there is always "Tea." There are always cakes, both big and little, to go with it. And there is always someone to say to the American traveler: "You don't have tea biscuits this size in America, do you? It is only the English housewife who makes them."

The American has to admit that cakes of such a size are not seen in this country, for the cakes, in question, are the the size of an ordinary bread and butter plate.

English cakes are seen the world over. It's English cake and tea for *tiffin* in India. It's English cake and tea in South Africa or Australia. As for Canada, one might as well be in London or the Low Country.

But some cakes seem more typically English than others. "Bath Buns," for instance, which are said to have taken their name from Bath, the famous watering place; "Banbury Cakes," originating with the "Banbury Cross" of nursery rhyme, in Oxfordshire; and "Rout Cakes," named after the fashionable evening party or "Rout" of early Victorian days, simply couldn't be anywhere but in England.

Bath Buns

8 cups flour sifted
3 tbsp. butter

Mix together

½ cup honey
¼ cup water

Mix

1½ cups sugar with
½ cup water. Stir until dissolved and let stand over night

Blend the butter into the flour. Make holes in the flour and fill them with the honey water and the sugar water. Knead into a smooth dough. Roll very thin, cut into small round cakes, brush lightly with water and bake at 400° F. until light brown.

Banbury Cakes

Mix together

1½ cups flour sifted   ½ cup butter
1 lb. currants   1 cup sugar
¼ cup candied orange peel
    chopped
¼ cup candied lemon peel
    chopped
1 tsp. allspice

Cream the butter and sugar together. Add the fruit mixture and blend well.

Roll puff paste very thin. Cut with a small oval cutter. Place a small spoon of the fruit mixture in the center of each cake, fold over and flatten out with the rolling pin. Sprinkle with powdered sugar and bake at 475° F. for ten to fifteen minutes.

Rout Cakes

1 lb. almonds blanched   2 cups sugar
grated rind of 1 lemon   4 egg yolks unbeaten

Dry the almonds in a warm oven. Pound them very fine and sift through a fine sieve. Mix with the sugar and lemon rind. Gradually add the egg yolks and mix into a smooth paste. Roll medium thin, using powdered sugar on the biscuit board. Cut into fancy shapes and bake at 400° F. until light brown.

Almond Paste

1 lb. almonds blanched $\frac{1}{2}$ lb. powdered sugar
2 tbsp. orange flower water 2 egg whites unbeaten

Shred the almonds and then roll them with a rolling pin until very fine. Gradually add the sugar, egg whites and orange flower water. Work the mixture into a smooth paste.

Spread little cakes with the paste and allow them to stand three days, then ice with raw icing.

Little Cakes to Ice

Dissolve in

1 cup milk
1 tsp. soda

1 cup butter
3 cups sugar
5 eggs unbeaten
4 cups flour sifted
grated peel and juice of 1 lemon

Cream the butter and sugar together. Add the eggs, one at a time, and mix well. Add the grated lemon rind and juice. Add the flour and milk alternately. Spread the batter thinly on a well buttered baking pan and bake at 350° F. for thirty minutes. Allow to cool in the pans, cut into tiny squares, and spread with almond paste. After the cakes have stood for three days ice with the following icing:

2 cups powdered sugar sifted
2 egg whites unbeaten
1 tsp. almond extract

Strain the egg whites through a medium fine sieve. Put them on a large platter and beat them with a flat egg beater. When the eggs begin to froth start adding the sugar. Beat steadily, adding the sugar gradually. Just before the last sugar is added add the almond extract. Allow to stand five minutes before spreading the cakes.

Rich Ginger Cake

This is a very old and much esteemed English cake. The original recipe called for the butter to be washed in rose water. This meant that the butter was broken into pieces, rose water was poured over it and the butter was worked in the water until soft. The rose water was then drained off, leaving a delightful flavor of roses.

In those old days housewives made their own rose water. In an old English cook book in the author's possession are these directions for making rose water: "Into a quart of pure spring water, stir four drops of Kissanlik Otto of Rose, and a large pinch of carbonate of Magnesia, and pass it through filter paper, or very fine muslin."

Sift together

4 cups flour
1 tbsp. Jamaica ginger
1 tsp. cinnamon
½ tsp. mace
1 tsp. cardamon

1½ cups butter
½ lb. powdered sugar
2 cups dark molasses
2 eggs slightly beaten

Mix with

¼ cup almonds blanched
and ground
½ cup citron sliced thin
½ cup candied orange peel
chopped
1 tsp. cardamon seed

Heat the butter, sugar and molasses together. When nearly cold, gradually add the eggs and flour mixture. Knead to a smooth dough, adding more flour if needed. Roll thin, cut into large cakes and bake at 400° F. until light brown.

English Tea Cakes

These are the favorite tea cakes served in a modest little cottage, graciously presided over by the typical British school teacher whose interest in humanity makes her enjoy nothing better than visiting over a cup of tea with her neighbors from across the well-trimmed hedge, or her American neighbors from across the Atlantic.

1 cup sugar
1 cup flour sifted
1 cup butter

1 cup currants
4 eggs unbeaten

Cream the butter and sugar together. Add the eggs, one at a time, and mix well. Blend in the flour and currants. Pour the batter into a shallow baking pan that has been lined with well-greased paper. Bake at 350° F. for thirty minutes. Cut into small squares while warm.

English Tea Biscuit

Sift together

8 cups flour
½ tsp. soda
½ tsp. nutmeg

1 cup butter
3 cups sugar
1 cup cream
3 eggs beaten slightly

Blend the butter into the flour. Add the eggs, sugar and cream and knead into a smooth dough. Roll thin and cut into large round cakes. Bake at 400° F. until light brown.

SCOTCH RECIPES

THE author remembers as one of her pleasantest childhood experiences the rare Sunday evenings in winter, when the father of the large family decided that he must have bannock he himself made.

It was a ritual, making those little water cakes of Scotland. The negro cook was called from the kitchen. She was given careful instructions about the amount of flour and salt to put in a big brown crock, to be brought along with the tripod and huge iron griddle. The cakes were baked over the coals on the broad dining room hearth.

The author looked about for bannock in Scotland and found it. It was not as good as the bannock of memory, but it was real Scotch bannock, she was told, the Scotch bannock that never changes from generation to generation.

Bannock

2 cups coarsely ground flour

$\frac{1}{2}$ tsp. salt
$\frac{1}{2}$ cup cold water

Add the water gradually to the flour and salt, using more if needed to make a stiff dough. Shape into thin round cakes with the hands. Bake on an ungreased griddle.

Belfasts

Sift together

1½ cups flour
½ tsp. salt
¼ tsp. soda
1 cup sugar

½ cup butter softened
¾ cup buttermilk
1 egg slightly beaten

Mix with

1½ cups graham flour
1 cup currants

Blend the butter into the flour. Mix in the milk and egg and knead into a smooth dough. Shape into thin cakes with the hands and bake at 400° F. for about thirty minutes.

Scotch Ginger Cake

Sift together

2 cups flour
½ tsp. soda
1 tsp. cinnamon
1 tsp. ginger

½ cup light molasses
½ cup butter
⅓ cup sugar
2 eggs well beaten

Heat the molasses, sugar and butter together until the butter is melted. Gradually add the eggs and mix well. Blend in the flour. Turn into a well greased baking pan to one-half inch thickness and bake at 350° F. for thirty minutes. Cut into small squares when cold.

Sour Cream Ginger Cake

Sift together

3 cups flour
1 tsp. soda
1 tsp. cinnamon
½ tsp. ginger
½ tsp. salt

Mix together

1 cup sugar
½ cup butter softened
1 cup light molasses
1 cup thick sour cream
2 eggs well beaten

Gradually add the flour to the molasses mixture. Bake as directed for Scotch Ginger Cake. Cut into small squares when cold.

Scones

Sift together

2 cups flour
1 tsp. salt
½ tsp. soda

¾ cup sour milk

Add enough milk to the flour to make a stiff dough. Shape into thin round cakes with the hands and bake on a griddle.

Spoon Currant Biscuit

Sift together

2 cups flour
1½ tsp. baking powder
½ tsp. salt

2 tbsp. lard
1 cup milk scant measure

Mix with

½ cup currants
2 tbsp. brown sugar

Blend the lard into the flour. Add the milk and mix quickly and lightly. Drop into small cakes and bake at 400° F. for fifteen minutes.

IRISH RECIPES

THE author went with Scotch friends to Ireland and partook of Irish Short Bread that might have been Scotch Short Bread, with the exception of nuts, brown sugar and ginger. It was equally rich, equally delicious. But the Scotchman likes his short bread free from salt and flavoring.

Both Irishman and Scotchman want strong black tea, freshly brewed and served with milk, just as the Englishman serves his tea with milk.

It is one of the most restful, most satisfying experiences of travel in the British Isles, to sit by a window in a quaint old tavern in Ireland and look out upon countrysides which have been unspoiled by the passing years.

Ireland is changing with the world changes that a modern age is effecting but there are still sights which are typically of the long ago. One may see a primitive two-wheeled cart drawn by a shaggy little donkey. The donkey is driven by a smiling-faced, blue-eyed, black-haired girl who is returning home with her cart load of empty milk cans. And if one is particularly fortunate, far down the road donkeys are jogging along, bearing their loads of peat fuel in crude baskets strapped across their backs.

Ginger Short Bread

Sift together

$1\frac{1}{2}$ cups flour
$\frac{1}{2}$ cup brown sugar
1 tsp. ginger
$\frac{1}{4}$ tsp. salt

$\frac{1}{2}$ cup butter softened
1 tbsp. cream

Blend the butter into the flour. Add the cream, a few drops at a time, and press the dough into a ball. Divide into halves, form into flat round cakes about the size of a saucer, prick with a fork, flute the edges and bake at 350° F. for thirty minutes.

Almond Short Bread

Mix together

2 cups flour sifted
½ cup almonds blanched
   and ground

½ cup butter softened
½ cup sugar
1 tbsp. water

Add the sugar and flour alternately to the butter, blending in the water as needed to make a stiff dough. Prepare and bake as directed for Ginger Short Bread.

Pound Cake

½ lb. butter creamed
2 cups pastry flour sifted
1⅔ cups sugar

5 eggs unbeaten
½ tsp. mace

Have a shallow baking pan greased, the oven ready and all the ingredients measured, as the mixing must be done by hand.

Add the sugar and mace to the butter and work until very light. Add one egg at a time and mix until thoroughly blended. Mix in the flour and turn at once into the baking pan. Bake at 350° F. for thirty minutes. Cut in small squares when cold.

GERMAN RECIPES

GERMAN housewives are noted the world over for their small cakes. Cookies are as characteristic of different localities as the colloquial speech. A cookie is recognized by its name. For instance, it may be "Low German" in name. If it is there is little difficulty in placing its origin. And thus, no liberties must be taken with the names of the cakes, which are a part of the traditions of a locality.

Drinking coffee and eating little cakes in Germany is a friendly, leisurely form of entertainment. The author recalls drinking coffee with a cosmopolitan group one afternoon, where there was such brilliant conversation the food was forgotten for a time. The host and hostess, a professor and his wife, knew the art of entertaining people from many lands, and doing it so graciously that Englishman, Frenchman, Austrian, Scandnivian and American met on a common ground of equal interest in those cultural subjects which are discussed by people of all countries.

The author finally compelled herself to note the kinds of small cakes. They were tiny, rich, carefully made cakes much like the cakes of all northern European countries.

Mandel Schnitte

(Almond Bars)

½ cup butter	1½ cups flour sifted
⅓ cup sugar	⅓ cup sugar
2 tbsp. milk	3 egg yolks well beaten

Cream the butter and sugar together. Add the egg yolks
and mix well. Add the flour and milk alternately and
knead into a soft dough. Roll thin and line a shallow pan
to a depth of one-half inch. Fill with the following mixture:

1½ cups almonds blanched   3 egg whites beaten dry
   and chopped fine   1 cup sugar

Gradually add the sugar to the egg whites. Fold in the
almonds. Fill the crust, sprinkle with sugar and bake at
350° F. for thirty minutes. Cool slightly and cut into strips
one inch wide and three inches long.

Mandel Kränze

(Almond Tea Cakes)

4 cups flour sifted   1½ cups butter creamed
3 egg yolks beaten seven
   minutes
1 cup sugar

Add the sugar to the butter and mix well. Gradually
add the eggs, beating all the time. Blend in the flour
and knead into a smooth dough. Roll very thin, cut into
small cakes, brush with egg white and sprinkle with sugar,
cinnamon and ground blanched almonds. Bake at 350° F.
to a light brown.

Mutze-Mandel

(Fried Almond Cakes)

2 cups flour sifted   ⅔ cup butter creamed
1 cup sugar   2 egg yolks unbeaten
½ lb. almonds blanched
   and ground

Add the eggs to the butter and mix well. Gradually add the sugar, then the flour and almonds. Shape into small balls and fry in hot fat to a golden brown.

Nuss Plätzchen

(Nut Cakes)

½ lb. almonds blanched
  and ground

½ lb. powdered sugar sifted
2 egg whites beaten stiff

Add the sugar gradually to the egg whites and beat fifteen minutes. Add the almonds. Turn out on a well floured board and roll to one-half inch thickness. Cut in small star shapes and bake at 325° F. for about thirty minutes.

Mandel Plätzchen

(Almond Cakes)

Sift together

3 cups flour
1½ tsp. baking powder

1½ lbs. brown sugar
½ lb. almonds blanched
  and ground
5 eggs unbeaten

Beat the eggs and sugar together until the eggs cease to be stringy. Add the almonds. Gradually add the flour and knead slightly. Roll to one-fourth inch thickness, cut into small cakes and bake at 350° F. until pale brown.

Mandel Stangen

(Almond Strips)

Sift together

2 cups flour
1 tbsp. baking powder
$\frac{1}{4}$ tsp. cinnamon

1 cup brown sugar
1 square chocolate grated
2 eggs beaten seven
   minutes
$\frac{1}{4}$ cup almonds blanched
   and ground
$\frac{1}{2}$ tsp. vanilla

Add the sugar gradually to the eggs and beat three minutes. Add the chocolate, then the flour and nuts. Press into a well-greased pan ten by ten inches and bake at 350° F. for thirty minutes. Cut into narrow strips while warm.

Mandel Küchen

(Almond Cakes)

1 cup flour sifted
1 cup sugar
1 cup almonds chopped

2 eggs unbeaten
$\frac{1}{2}$ tsp. vanilla

Add the sugar gradually to the eggs and mix well. Add the vanilla, the nuts and flour and mix into a smooth dough. Shape into little balls and bake at 350° F. until light brown.

Kaffee Gebäck

(Afternoon Coffee Bread)

Sift together

4 cups flour
2 scant tsp. cream of tartar

1 cup sugar
1 cup butter creamed
2 eggs unbeaten

Add the sugar gradually to the butter and beat until creamy. Add the eggs, one at a time, and mix well. Gradually add the flour and knead into a smooth dough. Roll thin, brush with egg white and sprinkle with sugar and ground almonds. Bake at 350° F. until light brown, fifteen to twenty minutes.

Haselnuss Makronen

(Hazelnut Macaroons)

$\frac{1}{2}$ lb. powdered sugar
   sifted
$\frac{1}{8}$ tsp. soda

$\frac{1}{4}$ lb. almonds blanched
   and chopped
$\frac{1}{4}$ lb. hazelnuts chopped
2 egg whites unbeaten

Add the sugar to the egg whites and stir for fifteen minutes. Add the soda and nuts and mix well. Turn on to a floured board and roll to one-half inch thickness. Cut into small round cakes and bake at 325° F. for thirty to forty minutes.

Butter-Ringe

(Rich Butter Cakes)

4 cups flour sifted
$\frac{1}{2}$ cup sugar
2 cups butter softened

$\frac{1}{2}$ tsp. almond extract
6 hard cooked egg yolks
   pressed through a sieve

Add the sugar gradually to the egg yolks and mix well. Blend in the butter, a little at a time. Gradually add the flour and knead slightly. Roll one-fourth inch thick and cut into strips one-fourth inch wide and four inches long.

Brush with egg white, sprinkle with cinnamon and coarse sugar and bake at 350° F. for ten to fifteen minutes.

Zucker Plätzchen

(Sugar Cookies)

Dissolve in

1 tbsp. hot water
1 tsp. soda
1 tsp. cinnamon

3 cups flour sifted
2 cups brown sugar
¾ cup butter creamed
2 eggs unbeaten

Add the sugar to the butter and cream ten minutes. Add the eggs, one at a time, and blend in well. Add the flour, the soda and cinnamon and knead into a smooth dough. Roll thin, cut into small cakes and bake at 400° F. until light brown.

Sandtörtchen

(Drop Cookies)

Mix and beat ten minutes

1 egg yolk
2 eggs

2 cups flour sifted five
   times
1 cup sugar sifted

Gradually add the sugar to the eggs and beat twenty minutes. Fold in the flour as lightly as possible. Drop into small cakes and bake at 325° F. for about ten minutes. Allow the cakes to cool before removing them from the pan with a thin-bladed knife.

Pfeffernüsse

(Christmas Cookies)

8 cups flour sifted
1½ cups dark molasses
1 cup water
peel one orange dried and
  powdered

¾ cup lard
1 tsp. each: cloves, allspice
  and cinnamon

Mix together all the ingredients but the flour and bring to a boil. Chill thoroughly, then gradually add the flour and knead into a smooth dough. Let the dough stand for two hours. Roll very thin and cut into medium sized round cakes. Bake at 350° F. until light brown and well dried out. The cookies are hard and will keep all winter.

Weihnachts Küchelchen

(Christmas Fruit Cookies)

Sift together

10 cups flour
3 tsp. soda
1 tsp. cardamon seed
  pounded

Mix with

1 cup almonds chopped
¼ lb. citron sliced thin
1 candied orange peel
  chopped

Mix together

1½ cups sugar
1½ cups dark corn syrup
1 cup lard melted
1 cup butter melted
grated rind 2 lemons

Blend the liquid into the flour and mix into a stiff dough, using more flour if needed. Roll thin, cut into small round cakes and bake at 350° F. for twelve to eighteen minutes.

Mandel Bretzel

(Almond Pretzels)

Mix together

2 cups flour sifted	1 cup butter creamed
½ lb. almonds ground	2 eggs unbeaten
	2 egg yolks unbeaten

Blend the eggs into the butter. Gradually add the flour and knead into a smooth dough. Divide into tiny balls, roll each piece into rolls four inches long and the size of a pencil and shape into pretzels. Brush with egg white, sprinkle with coarse sugar and bake at 350° F. until light brown.

Pretzel recipes should have no sugar if they are strictly German.

Makronen

(Cocoanut Macaroons)

Mix together

½ cup sugar	2 egg whites beaten stiff
1 tbsp. corn starch	1 heaping cup of cocoanut
	1 tsp. vanilla

Line a baking sheet with oiled paper well buttered.

Gradually add the sugar to the egg whites. Turn the mixture into a granite saucepan, set into a basin of boiling water and cook, stirring constantly, until the mixture begins to grain around the sides of the pan. Remove from the fire and mix in the cocoanut and flavoring. Drop the cakes with a coffee spoon. The macaroons should be the size of a penny. Bake at 400° F. until light brown.

Zimmt Sterne

(Cinnamon Stars)

1 lb. almonds blanched
and ground
1 lb. powdered sugar
sifted
1 lemon rind grated

6 egg whites beaten stiff
1 tsp. cinnamon

Wipe a baking sheet over with paraffine.

Add the sugar and lemon rind gradually to the egg whites. Remove one-fourth of the mixture to put on the center of the cookies. To the remaining mixture add the almonds and cinnamon. Roll, using powdered sugar to prevent sticking. Cut with a star-shaped cutter, place a small portion of the first mixture in the center of each cookie and bake at 350° F. until light brown.

Weihnachts Küchlein

(Cookies for Christmas Tree Decoration)

Sift together

3 cups flour
1 tsp. baking powder
½ tsp. soda
½ tsp. salt

½ cup lard softened
1 cup sugar
1 cup strong cold coffee
1 egg unbeaten

Add the sugar and egg to the fat and beat until light. Add the flour and coffee alternately and knead into a dough that will roll easily. Roll thin and cut into fancy shapes. Coat with chocolate or sprinkle with coarse sugar. Bake at 400° F. until light brown.

Anisplätzchen

(Anise Seed Cakes)

Sift together

1¼ cups flour
¼ cup cornstarch

1 cup sugar
4 eggs unbeaten
2 tbsp. anise seed

Mix the sugar and eggs together in a granite saucepan, set in a basin of boiling water and beat until the mixture becomes thick. Remove from the fire and beat until cold. Gradually add the flour and anise seed. Drop into small cakes and bake at 350° F. until light brown.

Leb Küchen

(Honey Cakes)

Mix together in a granite saucepan and bring to a slow boil. Set aside to cool.

1¾ cups honey
2 cups sugar

Sift together

5 cups flour
1 tbsp. cinnamon
1 tbsp. cloves

Mix with

1 cup citron chopped

3 eggs slightly beaten

Dissolve in

1 tbsp. water
2 tsp. soda

Gradually add the eggs, honey and soda to the flour. Knead into a smooth dough. Roll to one-fourth inch thickness, cut into small round cookies and bake at 325° F. for twenty minutes or longer, if needed to make the cakes very hard. These cakes are supposed to be dipped into coffee when eaten.

Weise Pfeffernüsse
(White Peppernuts)

Sift together

3 cups flour	2 cups sugar
2 tsp. baking powder	4 eggs unbeaten
1 tsp. cloves	grated rind of 1 lemon
1 tbsp. cinnamon	
½ tsp. nutmeg	

Mix with

1 cup thinly sliced citron

Gradually add the sugar to the eggs and beat ten minutes. Blend in the flour, adding more if needed to make a smooth dough. Roll thin, cut into small cookies and bake at 325° F. until light brown.

AUSTRIAN RECIPES

VIENNA, the city of music, of gaiety, of spendthrift tourists, seeking the pleasures that were not sated in Paris, that is the usual picture of Austria that is conjured up by the traveler.

But there is another picture for the traveler who wants to see more of the country than the cities and large continental hotels, for after all there is a great sameness in cities and hotels. That picture is Austrian homes.

The women of Austria are meticulous housekeepers and excellent cooks. They excel in the making of *risen cakes*.

Bundkuchen

(Coffee Cake)

4 cups flour sifted	3 egg yolks well beaten
¾ cup sugar	1 compressed yeast cake
1½ cups melted butter	1½ cups milk warmed
½ cup almonds blanched and chopped	

Break the yeast into the warm milk and let stand until it begins to foam. Add the eggs, sugar and butter. Gradually mix in the flour and beat for ten minutes. Let rise two hours. Again beat for ten minutes. Line a well-buttered pan with the nuts. Pour in the batter and let rise to double the bulk. Bake at 400° F. for about forty-five minutes. Cut into small squares and serve warm with afternoon coffee.

Toffen Kolatschen

(Cheese Cakes)

1 cup hot milk
⅓ cup butter
¼ cup sugar
¾ compressed yeast cake
   broken into
¼ cup warm water

2¾ cups flour sifted
½ tsp. salt
1 egg well beaten

Add the butter, sugar and salt to the milk. When tepid add the yeast, egg and flour. Beat ten minutes, adding more flour if needed to make a stiff batter. Let rise to double the bulk. Knead, adding flour to make a smooth dough. Let rise to double the bulk. Roll the dough thin, cut in four-inch squares.

Make a filling of

½ lb. cottage cheese (dry)
   pressed through a sieve
½ cup powdered sugar
   sifted

½ tsp. vanilla
2 egg yolks unbeaten

Mix the sugar, egg yolk, vanilla and cheese and beat until the egg yolks cease to be stringy.

Put a little of the cheese mixture in the center of each square. Fold over the four corners. Bake at 400° F. for about twenty minutes.

Kipfel

(Crescents)

2 cups boiled potatoes
   rubbed through a strainer
   and cooled

2 cups flour sifted
½ tsp. salt
1 cup butter

Blend the butter into the flour. Add the potatoes and salt and knead into a smooth dough. Roll, using more flour if needed. Fold the dough over and roll again. Repeat the process five times. Roll one-eighth inch thick and cut into three-inch squares.

Make a filling of:

¼ lb. walnuts ground   ¼ cup brown sugar
¼ cup butter softened

Blend the butter, sugar and walnuts into a smooth paste. Put a small amount of the mixture in the center of each square. Roll up the pieces of dough, beginning at a point. Bend into crescents and bake at 400° F. for about twenty minutes. Sprinkle with powdered sugar just before serving.

Sacher Torte

(Chocolate Torte)

1 cup flour sifted   ¼ lb. chocolate melted
2 cups butter   4 egg yolks well beaten
½ cup sugar   4 egg whites beaten stiff

Add the sugar to the butter and mix well. Add the chocolate and the egg yolks and beat until smooth. Gradually blend in the flour. When all is added, fold in the egg whites. Spread thinly in a well-buttered baking pan. Bake at 375° F. for about twenty minutes. Cut into little squares, stick two together with jam and ice with the following:

¼ lb. chocolate grated   2 cups sugar
¼ cup water   4 tsbp. water to use later

Cook the chocolate and water together until melted. Add the sugar and remaining water and cook to the soft ball stage. Beat to the consistency to spread.

RECIPES FROM HOLLAND

THE author thinks of Holland in tulip time. Tulips everywhere, and the fresh, pink-cheeked girls, in their quaint costumes, looking something like tulips themselves, as they go about their duties of making butter for the famous Thursday butter market at Middelburg.

Housewives of Holland use butter and cheese generously in their baking and the cakes they make are delicious.

Toffenstrudel

(Cheese Cakes)

2 cups flour sifted	1 egg well beaten
$\frac{1}{4}$ cup butter softened	$\frac{1}{2}$ tsp. salt
warm water to make a stiff dough	

Add the egg, butter and salt to the flour, then gradually mix in the water, blending the mixture into a stiff dough. Set aside for one hour.

Make a filling of:

$\frac{3}{4}$ cup butter	$\frac{1}{2}$ cup sugar
4 egg yolks well beaten	$\frac{1}{2}$ lb. Dutch cheese grated
grated rind of 1 orange	1 tbsp. cream

Blend the butter and sugar together until mixed but not soft. Add the cheese, orange rind, cream and egg and mix until thoroughly blended.

113

Roll the pastry into a thin long sheet. Spread the cheese mixture down the center. Fold the dough over, making a long roll. Seal the ends by pinching the dough securely over the filling and bake at 350° F. for forty-five minutes. Cut in slices when cold.

Poffertges

(Doughnuts)

1 cup flour sifted
¼ tsp. salt
1 tbsp. sugar

1 cup milk scalded
¼ cup butter
3 eggs unbeaten

Add the butter to the milk and stir until it melts. Add the flour and salt and beat until smooth. Cook, stirring constantly, until the dough leaves the sides of the pan. Remove from the fire and blend in the sugar and eggs. Shape into small balls and fry in deep fat until dark brown.

Beverwyks

(Spice Cakes)

Sift together

3 cups flour
1 tsp. each: cloves, allspice
    cinnamon

1 cup butter softened
1½ cups sugar
3 eggs unbeaten

Mix with

1 cup raisins chopped

Add the sugar and eggs to the butter and beat well. Add the other ingredients and mix quickly, using more flour to make a dough that will roll. Roll one-fourth inch thick, cut into small cakes and bake at 350° F. until light brown.

Platzen

(Drop Sponge Cakes)

Sift together five times

2 cups flour
1 tsp. each: cloves, cinnamon

2 cups powdered sugar
sifted
4 egg yolks beaten ten
minutes

Gradually add the sugar to the egg yolks. Fold in the flour, using just enough to make a dough that will drop from a spoon. Drop into small cakes and bake at 325° F. for about fifteen minutes.

DANISH RECIPES

DENMARK, with her low white-washed stone cottages, green meadows, and grazing cattle, fires the imagination of the traveler. There is something so substantial, so permanent, so utterly peaceful about the looks of it all that he wonders if Rollo the Dane might not have gazed out upon stone cottages and meadows and grazing cattle that looked much the same.

Then he arrives in Copenhagen and forgets the pastoral scenes in his fascination for the harbor, one of the most remarkable ports in the world, for such points of interest as Rosenborg Castle; or Our Lady's Church, with Thorvaldsen's Christ and the Twelve Apostles; or the "Regensen" and the "Round Tower" from whose heights a view of old town can be had that again brings forgetfulness of the present until he is rudely made aware of everyday surroundings by idle curiosity.

What in the world can all the leisurely strollers along the bench-lined street near the cathedral have in their little baskets? There is an old couple with a bigger basket. Why not follow them? They are looking for a place to sit in the shade. Ah, they are partaking of the contents of that mysterious basket.

It is strawberry season in Denmark. Everywhere along the streets people are sitting with their baskets, eating strawberries. A quaint custom the American thinks it. He feels a little superior until the sight of so many luscious berries brings a gnawing hunger. Then he thinks of tea, with little cakes to go with it, and possibly a dish of those huge ripe red strawberries.

He finds the cakes of Denmark are as choice as the strawberries. Neither could be better anywhere in the world.

Frisk Bröd

(Fresh Bread)

Sift together

6 cups flour   2 cups butter
1 cup sugar

Add the butter to the flour and continue working until the mixture is a paste. Make into rolls one-half inch in diameter and cut into cakes one and one-half inches long. Dip one side in slightly beaten egg white, then in sugar and chopped almonds. Bake at 350° F. until light brown.

Butterdeg

(Danish Puff Pastry)

2 cups flour sifted   6 tbsp. water
1 cup butter

Divide the butter into thirds. Flatten two of the pieces out on wax paper into thin cakes and set away in the refrigerator until needed.

Blend one-third of the butter into the flour. Gradually add the water and knead into a smooth dough. Roll to one-fourth inch thickness. Place one piece of the butter in the center of the dough, fold over the four sides, turn the dough folded side down on a well-floured board and roll to one-fourth inch thickness. Fold ends in one-third from each end and chill for twenty minutes. Repeat the process with the last piece of butter. After the last butter is added and the dough is chilled roll out the dough and fold in the ends. Chill for twenty minutes. Repeat the rolling and chilling process four times, always keeping the dough in a rectangular shape. Put away in the refrigerator for twenty-four hours. When using be careful not to knead the dough. Cut off small pieces, roll one-half inch thick, cut into narrow strips and shape into rings. Sprinkle with sugar and bake at 450° F. for twelve to fifteen minutes.

Kringler

(Pretzel)

Sift together

2 cups flour
1 tbsp. sugar
1 tsp. baking powder

½ cup butter
1 cup heavy cream
  whipped

Blend the butter into the flour. Mix in the cream and knead lightly into a soft dough. Roll thin, sprinkle with sugar and cut into strips one-fourth inch wide and six inches long. Form into pretzels and bake at 400° F. until light brown.

Hoide Kager

(Overnight Cookies)

2 cups flour sifted
1 cup sugar
¼ tsp. vanilla
⅛ tsp. lemon extract

1 cup butter
½ cup cream

Mix the flour and sugar. Blend in the butter until the mixture is mealy. Gradually add the cream and the flavoring. Shape into a roll one and one-half inch in diameter. Put away in the refrigerator overnight. Cut into thin slices and bake at 350° F. until light brown.

Jädekager

(Jew's Cakes)

Sift together

5 cups flour	1 cup sugar
1 tsp. carbonate ammonia	1½ cups butter
	2 eggs unbeaten

Cream the butter and sugar together. Add the eggs and mix well. Gradually add the flour and knead into a smooth dough. Roll thin, cut into small cakes, brush with egg white and sprinkle with sugar and chopped almonds. Bake at 275° F. to 300° F. until light brown.

Sprut Kager

(Cookie Press Cakes)

Sift together

2½ cups flour	1 egg slightly beaten
¾ cup sugar	1 cup butter

Blend the butter into the flour mixture. Add the egg and mix into a smooth dough. Make cookies with a cookie press into various shapes and bake at 300° F. until light brown.

Svendsker

(Ring Cookies)

Sift together

3 cups flour	1 cup butter
1 cup sugar	4 tbsp. water

Blend the butter into the flour. Add the water gradually and mix like pie crust. Shape into small rings with the hands and place on a floured board. Allow to stand in a cool place overnight. Brush with slightly beaten egg white and sprinkle with sugar just before baking. Bake at 350° F. until light brown.

Kleiner

(Fried Cakes)

4 cups flour sifted	5 egg yolks
1 cup sugar	1 egg
½ cup cream	

Add the sugar to the eggs and beat well. Add the flour and cream alternately and knead into a soft dough. Roll thin, cut into diamond shaped cakes, cut a diagonal slit in the center of each cake and draw one end through the slit. Cook in deep fat to a light brown.

Brunekager

(Brown Cakes)

1 cup butter
1 cup sugar
1 cup syrup (scant measure)
2 tbsp. molasses
1 egg unbeaten

Sift together

4 cups flour
1 tsp. soda
1 tsp. cinnamon
½ tsp. each: cloves, nutmeg, ginger

Cream the butter and sugar together. Add the egg, syrup and molasses and mix well. Gradually blend in the flour, adding more if needed to make a stiff dough. Make into small rolls and place in the refrigerator overnight. Slice thin and bake at 275° F. until light brown.

Sirupskager

(Molasses Cakes)

Sift together

4 cups flour
1 tsp. each: ginger, cloves, cinnamon

grated rind 1 orange
⅓ cup butter softened
1 cup sugar
1 cup molasses (light)
1 egg
1 tbsp. orange juice
1 tbsp. vinegar
1 tsp. soda

Mix the butter, sugar and egg together and beat until well blended. Add the orange juice and grated rind and the vinegar. Mix the soda into the molasses and add it and the flour alternately. Knead into a firm dough, adding more flour if needed. Roll thin, cut into fancy shapes, place one-half almond in the center of each cake and bake at 350° F. until light brown.

Ableskiver

(Apple Cakes)

Sift together

2 cups flour
½ tsp. salt

Dissolve in

2 tbsp. boiling water
1 tsp. soda

4 egg yolks unbeaten
4 egg whites beaten stiff
1½ cups buttermilk
½ cup cream

These cakes are baked in an iron apple cake griddle.

Add the buttermilk and cream gradually to the flour, beating until the batter is smooth. Add the egg yolks, one at a time, and beat well. Stir in the soda and fold in the egg whites lightly. Drop one-half teaspoon melted butter into each cup in the griddle, drop in one tablespoon of the batter and bake, turning over and over with a fork.

NORWEGIAN COOKIES

GERMANY, Denmark, Norway and Sweden have cookies so much alike it is difficult to tell one from the other if one is not very well versed in the little distinguishing marks of the cookery of a nation. Especially are the fried cakes of the Scandinavian countries similar. The fried cakes in the north of Norway are Christmas cookies.

The land of far north Norway holds a fascination for the traveler. Vivid pictures can be recaptured of a cottage nestled on the hillside overlooking a fjord cut deep into the mountainous sea coast. A lovely, serene-faced blond woman, wearing a hand-woven apron embroidered in exquisite design, works at a table. The table is scrubbed until it gleams white against the cottage wall which is decorated with quaint murals depicting a scene of ancient days. Men in strange belted blouses are manning a Viking ship. The prow of the ship, a marvelously carved head of a woman, is turned towards the open sea.

For generations the women of the cottage have made Christmas cakes, standing at the same scrubbed table, looking at the same Viking ship going to sea. They have all taken pride in doing their work so well that each generation of housewives equals or excels the generation before her.

Fattigman

(Fried Cakes)

Sift together

4 cups flour
1 tsp. cinnamon

1 cup sugar
6 egg yolks well beaten
4 tbsp. heavy cream
1 tsp. cardamon seed

Add the sugar to the egg yolks and mix well. Add the cream and cardamon seed and blend in the flour gradually. Knead slightly and let stand in the refrigerator overnight. Roll very thin and cut into diamond shaped cakes. Cut a slit in the top point of the diamond, draw the opposite point through the slit and fry in deep fat to a light brown. Drain on unglazed paper.

Scun Cakka

(Sand Cakes)

Sift together

2½ cups flour
1 tsp. cinnamon

1 cup butter
1 cup sugar
1 egg well beaten
15 cardamon seed
      powdered

Cream the butter, sugar and cardamon seed together. Add the egg and mix well. Gradually blend in the flour and knead into a soft dough, adding more flour if needed. Press the dough into tiny fluted pans to the thickness of thin pie crust. Bake at 400° F. for about ten minutes.

Sand Bakels

(Tea Cakes)

Sift together

3 cups flour
½ tsp. baking powder

1 cup butter unsalted
1 cup sugar
1 tbsp. cream
1 egg unbeaten

Cream the butter and sugar together, add the egg and mix well. Add the flour and cream and knead into a soft dough. Roll thin, cut into small cakes, sprinkle with sugar and bake at 400° F. until light brown.

Krumkaki

(Rolled Wafers)

The rolled wafer of Norway and Sweden is regarded by many travelers as the choicest small cake made by northern European housewives. The Scandinavian housewife prides herself upon the perfection of her rolled wafers. The author had "Tea" in the household of an internationally known Scandinavian woman, who told her, with just pride, that she herself had made all the delectable little cakes served that afternoon.

These paper thin rolled cookies are baked in a special wafer iron which can be purchased in most large cities in America.

Sift together

1 cup flour (heaping)
½ tsp. cinnamon

1 cup butter melted
1 cup sugar
4 eggs well beaten

Add the sugar gradually to the eggs and beat three minutes. Add the butter, then gradually add the flour. Put a teaspoon of the batter into the wafer iron. Cook over a medium heat for one to two minutes. Roll while the cookie is hot. These cakes are fragile and must be handled with great care.

Krom Krage

(Cream Cakes)

2¼ cups flour sifted five
    times
1½ cups thick cream

3 egg yolks well beaten
½ cup sugar

Add the egg yolks to the sugar and beat well. Add the cream and flour alternately. Bake as directed for Krumkaki.

Berlinerkranzer

(Egg Cakes)

3½ cups flour sifted
1 cup butter softened
½ cup sugar

2 hard cooked egg yolks
2 egg yolks unbeaten

Rub the sugar into the cooked egg yolks until the mixture is a paste. Gradually blend in the raw egg yolks. Add the flour and butter alternately and knead into a smooth dough. Form into little rings with the hands, brush with egg white and sprinkle with sugar. Bake at 400° F. for about ten minutes.

Bertines Mandelbund

(Almond Cakes)

Mix together

3 cups flour sifted
¼ cup almonds blanched
and ground

1 cup butter creamed
1 cup sugar
¼ tsp. almond extract

Mix together and beat
ten minutes

1 tbsp. water
3 eggs

Mix the butter, sugar and flavoring together and beat ten minutes. Add the flour and eggs alternately and knead to a smooth dough, adding more flour if needed. Shape into small balls and bake at 400° F. for eighteen to twenty minutes.

SWEDISH COOKIES

COOKIES in Sweden! Was there ever anything like the display of interesting cakes to be found everywhere in the Land of the Midnight Sun? The Swedish housewife cherishes her small cake recipes as a birthright, handed down to her through many ages of meticulous housewifery.

All classes in Sweden eat cookies and drink coffee every day. No matter when two friends meet they partake of small cakes and sip strong coffee from tiny cups. The coffee is served with thick cream and there is sugar to be used with the last half cup.

The traveler is impressed with the little shops where cookies are sold. If she is an American housewife, who is forever looking for something different, she may be tempted to buy a great bag of small cakes and try sampling them all, hoping to discover the secret of their excellence.

But to appreciate the real culinary art which goes into cookie making one must go to "Tea," where the meal is served with all the formality which makes it so different from the informal meal enjoyed in American households.

The author went to "Tea" in many charming Swedish homes. She was sadly lacking in manners at first. Later she learned the little points of etiquette which must be rigidly followed.

"Tea" at a famous medieval castle, presided over by a Baroness who is a modern woman, busy with many social and economic problems, was the pleasant culmination of tea drinking in a country that holds culinary art as woman's highest achievement.

128

The tea table was drawn close to a sofa. It was a grotesquely long sofa, magnificently carved, and exquisitely upholstered in hand woven damask.

The Baroness had a twinkle in her eyes when she explained: "The sofa was made especially for the castle in the long ago days when the Baron and His Majesty the King were such good friends that elaborate entertaining was always going on. The place of honor was to the right of the hostess. The other guests sat according to their rank. The ones who had no place on the sofa were very unhappy about it. So the tactful Baron had a sofa made so long that many ladies of high rank could sit side by side as they drank their tea."

Still the guest of honor sits to the right of the hostess on the sofa. The other guests sit around the table.

The table was spread with a hand-made lace cloth from the province of Jamtland. The tea service was handsome hand wrought silver, very old, very artistic in design. Before each guest was a small plate on which was placed a round lace finger doilie no larger than the center of the plate. On the doilie rested the teacup and saucer. To the right of the plate was a small fork and a teaspoon.

The guests removed their cups and saucers and placed them to the right of the plates. They put the finger doilies in their laps. They were ready for tea.

There is an etiquette in serving the food. The routine is: a small fancy roll for the first food eaten. This is followed by *soft* cake. The *soft* cake is usually a sponge cake filled with almond paste and whipped cream. Then come the *hard* cookies.

The guest of honor must take some of everything. It is the epitome of bad manners for her to fail to take one of each kind of the small hard cakes. Frequently her plate is piled high with an assortment, which is disconcerting to the

American. But the conventions must not be disregarded; for other guests must not take anything which the guest of honor has failed to take.

The hostess pours and the tea is passed by the guests. She pours a tiny amount into her own cup to see that it is just right. Then she pours a cup and passes it to the guest of honor. The other cups are passed to her left. The guest of honor passes no tea. Cream and sugar is then passed.

A maid, in conventional black uniform with sheer white cap and apron, passes the food. The formal service is similar to that in America. Food is passed to the left. The guest of honor is served first, then the hostess, then the other guests.

Eating is leisurely engaged in. It is proper to stay not longer than an hour or an hour and a quarter. That time is spent at the tea table. When the meal is over the guests leave, unless the hostess gives a special invitation for the guests to remain longer for some definite further entertainment.

The author was invited many times to stay longer to see "Collections." Swedish women are great *collectors*. Their collections may be ancient Swedish textiles, or modern Swedish glass, or ivories from China, or etchings from the famous etchers of the past and present. Whatever the collection is it is as excellent of its kind as was the food served by the soft-footed maid, who never made a false move.

Käffebrod

(Tea Biscuit)

This is the kind of biscuits that were served as the first food at "Teas."

Sift together

7 cups flour	$\frac{1}{2}$ cup butter melted
1 tsp. salt	$\frac{1}{2}$ cup sugar
$\frac{1}{8}$ tsp. each: nutmeg, cardamon, cinnamon	2 egg yolks well beaten
	2 cups milk lukewarm
	$\frac{1}{2}$ cup sultana raisins
	$\frac{1}{4}$ cup currants
	1 compressed yeast cake broken into $\frac{1}{4}$ cup lukewarm water

Mix the flour, raisins and currants. Mix the butter, sugar and egg together and beat well, then add the milk. Pour the yeast into the flour. Gradually add the milk mixture and blend into a smooth dough. Knead until the dough ceases to stick to the hands. Let rise in a warm place for six or eight hours, or to double the bulk. Knead again. Divide into small biscuits and roll them thin. Cover with almond paste or heavy sweet apple sauce, roll the dough over the filling and seal the edges. Bake at 450° F. for twenty to thirty minutes.

To make the almond filling

1 cup almonds blanched and ground	1 cup sugar
heavy cream	

Mix the almonds and sugar. Work in the cream, a few drops at a time, until the mixture is a paste.

Sprit Kakor

(Butter Cakes)

Swedish housewives have borrowed the use of baking powder from America. The baking powder is even imported from America. Cookie recipes with baking powder are an indication that they are modern Swedish.

Sift together

3 cups flour
1 tsp. baking powder

1 cup butter creamed
1 cup sugar
2 eggs unbeaten

Add the sugar to the butter and mix well. Add the eggs, one at a time, and mix well. Add the flour gradually and mix into a smooth dough. Put the dough through the cookie press and form the cakes into small rings. Bake at 400° F. until light brown.

Sprit Kransar

(Swedish Cookies)

7 cups flour sifted
1¾ cups sugar
6 egg yolks well beaten

2 cups butter creamed
grated rind ½ lemon

Add the sugar and egg yolks gradually to the butter and mix well. Add the lemon rind and blend in the flour, using two knives to mix the dough.

Put the dough through the cookie press, grinding it out in long strips on the biscuit board. Cut the strips in even lengths and form into small circles. Bake at 350° F. until light brown.

Lisa-Kakor

(Elizabeth Cookies)

Sift together

1 cup flour	5 cups flour sifted
2 tsp. baking powder	1½ cups sugar
	1 tbsp. butter melted
	1 tsp. orange juice
	3 eggs well beaten
	citron cut in strips

Gradually add the sugar to the eggs, beating all the time. Add the butter and orange juice and again mix well. Blend in five cups of flour, then add the flour and baking powder and knead to a smooth dough. Roll thin, cut into small cookies, place a strip of citron on each, and bake at 400° F. until light brown.

Kanelbröd

(Toasted Cakes)

Sift together

4 cups flour	1 cup butter
2 tsp. baking powder	3 eggs well beaten
1 tsp. cinnamon	
1 cup sugar	

Blend the butter into the flour. Mix in the eggs as lightly and quickly as possible. Roll into two long loaves. Bake at 350° F. for about thirty minutes. When baked cut slices one inch thick diagonally across the loaf. Return to the oven and toast to a golden brown.

Ess Kakor

(S-Cookies)

Sift together

10 cups flour

3 tsp. baking powder

1½ cups butter creamed

1¼ cups sugar

5 egg yolks unbeaten

Add the sugar to the butter and beat until very light. Add one egg yolk at a time and continue beating until the eggs are well mixed. Gradually add the flour and knead to a smooth dough. Form into S shaped cookies with the hands, dip into coarse sugar, and bake at 400° F. until light brown.

Mändelhorns

(Almond Crescents)

2 cups almonds blanched
   and chopped

3½ cups sugar

1 tsp. vanilla

5 egg whites beaten stiff

Mix the almonds and sugar. Add the vanilla and fold in the egg whites. Form into small crescent shaped cakes and bake at 275° F. for thirty minutes.

Spet Caka

(The Cake of Scania)

Spet Caka is the cake baked on a log. And in the old days the cake was actually baked on an oak log fitted with a handle like a spit of olden times. Now housewives have a piece of equipment which makes the work much simpler.

But still the cake is baked before hot coals. The person who turns the *spindle* must be very dextrous, for the success of the cake depends upon the perfection of baking.

Spet Caka is the cake of Scania, the southern province of Sweden. It has the place of honor among all the cookies at the two great celebrations of the year, Christmas and Midsummer Day. Making the Spet Caka is an important event. All the women of the family help with the beating of the eggs and the baking.

The author had the privilege of seeing one of these famous cakes one Midsummer Day in Scania. That cake was a work of art. It stood about three feet high and was topped by a smaller cone which was used as a container for corn flowers. It was the centerpiece of the long tea table placed on the lawn, near the Maypole. There were dozens of other cakes on the table. They were eaten. The Spet Caka was left untouched.

It was not until the midnight supper that the cake was eaten. The hostess served the cake by breaking off generous sized pieces and passing a piece at a time to the guests. It was delicious. But how was it made? A colonel of His Majesty's Army was at the same table with the author. It was he who found out how the festive cake was made. And it came to light too that the cake was a part of the menu for the birthday celebrations of famous or important people.

70 egg yolks unbeaten	$3\frac{1}{2}$ lbs. sugar
70 egg whites beaten stiff	$3\frac{1}{2}$ lbs. potato flour

Beat the egg yolks and sugar together for one hour. Fold in the egg whites, then lightly fold in the potato flour. The dough is spread thinly on the utensil used for baking.

RUSSIAN RECIPES

It is a delightful trip from Stockholm to Riga, the first stop in Russia. One goes to Visby, that island in the Baltic, famed in Viking times as the first *port of call* between the mainland of Europe and Asia. One stops in Finland next, but the artists, the writers, the musicians, the mistresses of the castles one meets are so much like the Scandinavian people, with such similar food, no especial interest is taken in searching for little cakes that are different. So one goes on to Russia, determined to see all of Russia possible, old Russia as well as new Russia.

There is the chorus singing in the Volga country that is not surpassed in any nation. There is the hand weaving of fine linens, and the exquisite embroideries done by women who love beauty. And there are the great brass samovars of coffee, heated by coals put into a pipe in the center of the urn. There is boiling water too, to make tea in one's own teapot that is tucked somewhere in the hand luggage, and there are little cakes. They are typically Russian cakes.

Drachona
(Russian Cakes)

2½ cups flour sifted   1 cup milk
¼ cup powdered sugar
   sifted
2 tbsp. butter melted
½ tsp. salt
2 egg yolks well beaten

Beat the butter, sugar and eggs together and add the salt. Blend in the flour and milk alternately. Spread thinly in a well greased pan and bake at 350° F. for about thirty minutes. Cut into small squares when cold.

Tvorojiniki

(Cream Cheese Cakes)

Sift together

3½ cups flour	½ lb. cream cheese
¼ tsp. nutmeg	¼ cup melted butter
½ tsp. salt	3 eggs unbeaten

The cream cheese is made by putting clabbered milk into a muslin bag, hanging it in a cool place, and allowing it to drip for twelve hours.

Mix the cheese, butter, eggs and two cups of flour together. Rub the mixture through a sieve and then work in the remaining flour. Mold into small flat cakes and cook in boiling water. Drain on a cloth and sprinkle with sugar.

Sirniki

(Fried Cheese Cakes)

3 lbs. cottage cheese (dry curds)	4 eggs unbeaten
3 tbsp. butter softened	
1 heaping tbsp. flour sifted	
1 tbsp. sugar	

The cheese should be very dry.

Rub the cheese through a sieve. Add the eggs, one at a time, and mix well. Add the other ingredients and again mix well. Shape into small cakes, roll in flour, and fry in butter.

Smettanick

(Sour Cream Tarts)

1½ cups flour sifted   1 egg yolk well beaten
½ cup butter   ½ tsp. salt

Blend the flour, butter and salt together until the mixture is mealy. Add the egg yolk and knead into a smooth dough, adding a few drops of ice water if needed. Beat with a steak beater until the dough blisters. Roll very thin and cut into three-inch squares. Make a filling as follows:

1½ cups almonds blanched   thick sour cream
   and ground   2 tbsp. jam
1 egg yolk unbeaten   2 tbsp. powdered sugar

Work the powdered sugar into the almonds, adding a few drops of cream and egg yolk as needed. Add the jam gradually. When the mixture is finished it should be a paste. Place a spoonful of the filling in the center of a square of pastry, brush the edges with cold water, place another square on top and seal the edges by fluting them. Brush the tarts with egg white, sprinkle with sugar and bake at 450° F. until brown.

RECIPES FROM TURKEY

TURKEY was a country of smart traders long before America was anything but a wilderness with nomad Indian tribes following great bison herds, and hunting and fishing.

The traveler recalls bazaars in Turkey where Oriental wares are displayed so temptingly that it takes will power to resist making room for brasses in the battered old suit case, by rolling last year's silk dresses into neat packages and tossing them out to the first attractive girl seen by the roadside, on the long journey to the next village.

One is equally interested in the coffee and cakes, for one recalls that coffee in colonial America was Turkish coffee, made after the Turkish method, and used only by those settlers who could afford luxuries.

Turkish coffee is made by putting equal parts of finely ground coffee and sugar together in an open copper kettle and adding sufficient water to cover the ingredients. The pot is then set on a brisk fire and allowed to come to a boil. The syrup is immediately removed from the fire and allowed to cool slightly. The boiling process is repeated two more times before the syrup is ready to drain from the coffee grounds. A little rose water is added to the coffee when it is served.

Rahat el Halkum

(Turkish Paste)

4 cups sugar
1½ cups water
1 cup almonds blanched
  and chopped
1 drop attar of roses

½ cup cornstarch
1 tbsp. lemon juice

Cook the sugar and water to a heavy syrup. Mix the lemon juice, nuts and cornstarch together and blend the mixture slowly into the syrup, beating well to keep the starch from lumping. Cook until clear, stirring all the time. Add the attar of roses. Turn the paste out on a board covered with powdered sugar. Spread to one-half inch thickness. Cut in small squares when cold.

Beurrik

(Cheese Sticks)

½ lb. Gruyere cheese
3 tbsp. thick white sauce

puff pastry

Cook the cheese and white sauce together until thick. Chill thoroughly and shape into three-inch rolls the size of a pencil. Roll the puff paste very thin. Wrap the cheese in strips of pastry and fry in hot fat. Drain on brown paper.

Baklava

(Honey Squares)

Sift together
1 cup whole wheat flour
¼ tsp. salt

Mix together
1 egg slightly beaten
1 tbsp. water

Blend the egg into the flour and knead into a smooth dough. Beat the dough with a steak beater until it blisters. Divide into tiny pieces and roll as thin as paper. Allow to stand for one hour to dry out.

Make a filling as follows:

Boil to a thick syrup	1 cup pistachio nuts
$\frac{1}{2}$ cup honey	$\frac{1}{2}$ cup melted butter
$\frac{1}{2}$ cup water	

Fill a baking pan three-fourths full with layers of pastry, sprinkled with nuts. Pour the melted butter over the pastry and bake at 450° F. for twenty minutes. Pour the hot syrup over the pastry and allow to cool before cutting it into small squares.

INDIAN RECIPES

THE fortunate American traveler in India has English friends who extend the delightful hospitality of British India, and initiate him into some of the ways of that vast fascinating land of incredible wealth and pomp, beauty of art objects created by craftsmen: Cashmere shawls and exquisite rugs, pottery and brasses, mosaics and jewelry, in contrast to incredible jungles infested with fierce beasts and reptiles.

He enjoys strange dishes made with curry so different from the powdered kind American housewives know that it is hardly recognizable. He learns what real Indian chutney is, and he becomes acquainted with the lusciousness of melons and fruits; but while he is enjoying these delicious foods he looks about for cakes. He must be satisfied with finding two or three.

Paratha

(Whole Wheat Biscuit)

Sift together

2 cups whole wheat flour   water to make a stiff
½ tsp. salt   dough

Mix the ingredients into a stiff dough. Knead until smooth, roll into very thin round cakes and bake on a griddle.

Goolgoola

(Fried Cakes)

Sift together

2 cups flour
1 tsp. cinnamon

1 cup sugar
1 cup milk
$\frac{1}{2}$ cup butter
1 cake compressed yeast
dissolved in
1 tbsp. warm water

Mix the flour and milk together to a smooth paste. Add the sugar and butter and cook, stirring constantly. When thick and clear remove from the fire and cool to tepid. Work in the yeast and allow to set until thoroughly cold. Make into small balls and fry in butter.

JAPANESE RECIPES

THE American traveler, if he thinks about it at all, expects to have rice cakes whenever he has tea in Japan. He draws his conclusions from the tins of paper-thin rice cakes he purchases in a shop anywhere from San Francisco to Timbuctoo. Rice cakes, or any other cakes are hard to find at Afternoon Tea in Japan.

Drinking tea in Japan is a ceremony. The "Tea Ceremony" is so difficult to learn one goes to school a whole year before it is thoroughly mastered.

The American traveler in Japan is told by friends of the Diplomatic Service that there is only one safe code of etiquette for the American woman to follow when going to "Tea" in Japan. The simple rules she must follow are easily conformed to. She must slip off her shoes at the door. The Japanese hostess will probably supply her with sandals which she must put on. Then she must be sure to take the right position at the tiny tea table. Kneel, sit back upon the heels, and keep the body erect. The cup, the diplomatic friend advises, should be held in the cupped left palm. It is lifted with the right hand and the tea is sipped.

This much of the ceremony was simple enough. But the food that went with that particular "Tea" was difficult. Soy beans had been cut in thick and thin, big and little pieces, then roasted, much as we salt almonds. They had a pleasing flavor, and all the pieces somehow tasted a little different. But they were a poor substitute for tea cakes.

"Are toasted soy beans all one gets for tea?" the diplomatic friend was asked.

"The American lady would like cakes with her tea," he told the attendant in the little Tea House.

A queer sort of sweet was brought. *Yokan* it is called.

Yokan

(A Sweet Made of Beans)

2 lbs. red beans	4 cups sugar
2 ounces gelatine soaked in	
¼ cup cold water for ten	
minutes	

Boil the beans three hours. Rub them through a sieve. Add the sugar and gelatin and cook slowly six to eight hours. Turn into a shallow pan and cut into small squares when cold.

CHINESE RECIPES

COOKING in China is an art. Culinary secrets are handed down like family traditions. There is no such thing in China, the author was told, as a cook book. And though the American and the British who make their homes in the Land of the Lotus Flower have the Anglo Saxon urge for accuracy they make little progress with their native cooks. Recipes are still not written, they are remembered.

Sweets have a definite place in the art of dining. There are many kinds of cakes. Some seem strangely flavored to the foreign palate. Some are a national institution like the Moon Cakes. Some are so much like the sweets of other lands that one wonders if Anglo Saxon accuracy has not made a little progress after all.

Wt Beng

(Moon Cakes)

Moon Cakes have been connected with the Festival of the Eighth Moon since ancient times. This festival is called the moon's birthday. It comes at the time of the Harvest Moon when the full moon rises soon after sunset. The moon is the object of worship, and during the three days marked by out-door holiday making, she is called the Queen of Heaven. Women, in their moon worship, offer Moon Cakes to the Queen of Heaven. These cakes are really little tarts very much like the English mince

146

meat tarts. They are tiny, dainty cakes with a crescent cut into the top crust.

1 cup Chinese dates chopped	1 cup brown sugar
1 cup green dried plums chopped	½ cup red wine
6 red fruit chopped	2 cups chopped boiled beef
¼ cup walnut meats chopped	½ cup chopped suet
¼ cup preserved ginger	12 lotus seed
½ cup pine nuts	1 tsp. ginger
	½ tsp. salt

Mix all the ingredients together and cook slowly for one hour. Cool before using.

Line small tart pans with pie crust rolled very thin. Fill the pans three-fourths full, cover with a top crust in which a crescent has been cut and bake at 475° F. for twenty to thirty minutes.

Hang Yan Beng

(Almond Cakes)

Sift together

1 cup rice flour
½ cup brown sugar

⅓ cup butter softened
water if needed

Mix with

2 cups almonds blanched and ground

Blend the butter into the flour mixture. Add a few drops of water if needed to hold the dough together. Shape into small balls with the hands. Bake at 350° F. until light brown.

Tsoi Yan Beng

(Sesame Cakes)

Sift together

¼ cup flour
¼ cup rice flour
¼ cup sugar
1 tsp. baking powder

½ cup milk
2 tbsp. butter melted
1 egg slightly beaten
2 tbsp. sesame seed

Gradually add the milk, butter and egg to the flour and mix into a smooth batter. Spread thinly on a well-buttered pan, sprinkle with sesame seed and bake at 350° F. for fifteen to twenty minutes. Cut into small squares when cold.

Kai Tan Ko

(Sponge Cake)

Sift together five times

1 cup cake flour
1 cup sugar

5 eggs beaten thirty minutes
1 tsp. lemon juice

Gradually fold the flour and sugar into the eggs, mixing as little and as lightly as possible. Add the lemon juice. Turn into a buttered mould, cover tightly and steam in a steamer for forty-five minutes. Cool in the mould.

Fa Shang Bo

(Peanut Puff)

1 lb. puffed rice
2 cups malt syrup
½ cup sesame seed

2 cups peanuts
2 cups brown sugar

Bake the sesame seed in a 350° F. oven for five minutes. Cook the sugar and syrup together until it makes a hard ball in cold water. Keep the syrup hot. Mix the rice, peanuts and part of the sesame seed in the syrup. Pour into a buttered pan and press down evenly. Sprinkle the rest of the seed on top and set in a cool place for five minutes. Remove from the pan and cut in thin slices.

Mat Nga Tong Beng Tsai

(Malt Squares)

Cook together until the
   syrup threads and keep
   hot

1 cup malt syrup	whole kernels of water-
1 cup brown sugar	melon seed
	noodles

To make the noodles:

3 eggs slightly beaten	2 tbsp. water
flour to make a stiff dough	

Gradually add flour to the eggs and water until the mixture is stiff. Knead for thirty minutes, roll very thin and cut into one-fourth inch strips. Allow to dry one day then cut into one-fourth inch squares. Fry the noodles to a golden brown in hot peanut oil. Pour the syrup over enough of the noodles to hold together in a firm mass. Stir lightly and press in a one-inch-deep pan. Sprinkle with whole kernels of watermelon seed. Cut in squares while still warm.

MEXICAN RECIPES

"AROUND the World Making Cookies" should end in San Francisco, after the journey from China, but a whim takes the author to Mexico.

Mexico City, the city literally in the clouds, has an Old World charm that is not in keeping with the national corn cake of the land. But *tortillas* are pleasing to the palate because of their plainness.

True tortillas are made from dried corn soaked in lye. The lye is washed off and the husks removed from the corn. It is then dried and ground in a *metate*. The meal is coarse and of a pleasing flavor.

Tortillas
(Corn Cakes)

1 cup corn meal   1 cup boiling water
1 tsp. salt

Mix the ingredients together into a smooth paste. Allow to cool. Shape into small flat cakes with the hands and bake slowly on an ungreased griddle until crisp and brown.

Bunuelos
(Fried Cakes)

Mix and bring to a boil.   Sift together
  Remove from the fire

1 cup water   1 cup flour
1 tsp. butter   1 tsp. baking powder

Gradually add the flour to the boiling water. Beat until cold. Knead into a smooth dough, using a little flour to keep from sticking. Make into small balls and fry in hot fat. Drain on unglazed paper and sprinkle with sugar.

"Bien Me Sabe"

(Cocoanut Squares)

These delicious cakes are apparently known by no other name, which seemed so strange to the author that she inquired of several people. "No," the answer came, "we call them, *Bien Me Sabe.*"

Meat of 1 large cocoanut   1 cup milk
   grated

Mix the milk and cocoanut and heat slowly to boiling. Cool and squeeze through a cheese cloth bag. Use the milk to make a custard.

To make the custard:

cocoanut milk   4 egg yolks well beaten
4 tbsp. sugar

Mix the sugar with the egg yolks. Add the milk and cook over simmering water until it thickens. The custard should be stirred constantly. Allow to cool. Coat small squares of sponge cake with the custard, ice and cover with grated cocoanut.

To make the icing:

4 egg whites beaten stiff
8 tbsp. sugar

Gradually add the sugar to the egg whites, beating all the time. Let stand three minutes before spreading the cakes.

To make the sponge cake:

Mix together and beat
  seven minutes

6 egg yolks	1 cup sugar sifted
1½ tbsp. water	1 cup cake flour sifted five times
	1 tsp. lemon extract
	6 egg whites beaten seven minutes

Add half the sugar to the egg yolks and beat three minutes. Add the rest of the sugar to the egg whites and beat three minutes. Fold the egg whites into the egg yolks. Fold in the flour as lightly as possible and add the flavoring. Turn the batter into a shallow ungreased pan and bake at 325° F. for thirty minutes. Allow to cool before cutting into small squares.

INDEX

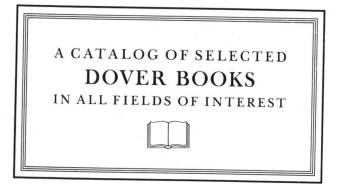

A CATALOG OF SELECTED
DOVER BOOKS
IN ALL FIELDS OF INTEREST

A CATALOG OF SELECTED DOVER BOOKS IN ALL FIELDS OF INTEREST

DRAWINGS OF REMBRANDT, edited by Seymour Slive. Updated Lippmann, Hofstede de Groot edition, with definitive scholarly apparatus. All portraits, biblical sketches, landscapes, nudes. Oriental figures, classical studies, together with selection of work by followers. 550 illustrations. Total of 630pp. 9⅛ × 12¼.
21485-0, 21486-9 Pa., Two-vol. set $25.00

GHOST AND HORROR STORIES OF AMBROSE BIERCE, Ambrose Bierce. 24 tales vividly imagined, strangely prophetic, and decades ahead of their time in technical skill: "The Damned Thing," "An Inhabitant of Carcosa," "The Eyes of the Panther," "Moxon's Master," and 20 more. 199pp. 5⅜ × 8½. 20767-6 Pa. $3.95

ETHICAL WRITINGS OF MAIMONIDES, Maimonides. Most significant ethical works of great medieval sage, newly translated for utmost precision, readability. Laws Concerning Character Traits, Eight Chapters, more. 192pp. 5⅜ × 8½.
24522-5 Pa. $4.50

THE EXPLORATION OF THE COLORADO RIVER AND ITS CANYONS, J. W. Powell. Full text of Powell's 1,000-mile expedition down the fabled Colorado in 1869. Superb account of terrain, geology, vegetation, Indians, famine, mutiny, treacherous rapids, mighty canyons, during exploration of last unknown part of continental U.S. 400pp. 5⅜ × 8½. 20094-9 Pa. $6.95

HISTORY OF PHILOSOPHY, Julián Marías. Clearest one-volume history on the market. Every major philosopher and dozens of others, to Existentialism and later. 505pp. 5⅜ × 8½. 21739-6 Pa. $8.50

ALL ABOUT LIGHTNING, Martin A. Uman. Highly readable non-technical survey of nature and causes of lightning, thunderstorms, ball lightning, St. Elmo's Fire, much more. Illustrated. 192pp. 5⅜ × 8½. 25237-X Pa. $5.95

SAILING ALONE AROUND THE WORLD, Captain Joshua Slocum. First man to sail around the world, alone, in small boat. One of great feats of seamanship told in delightful manner. 67 illustrations. 294pp. 5⅜ × 8½. 20326-3 Pa. $4.95

LETTERS AND NOTES ON THE MANNERS, CUSTOMS AND CONDITIONS OF THE NORTH AMERICAN INDIANS, George Catlin. Classic account of life among Plains Indians: ceremonies, hunt, warfare, etc. 312 plates. 572pp. of text. 6⅛ × 9¼. 22118-0, 22119-9 Pa. Two-vol. set $15.90

ALASKA: The Harriman Expedition, 1899, John Burroughs, John Muir, et al. Informative, engrossing accounts of two-month, 9,000-mile expedition. Native peoples, wildlife, forests, geography, salmon industry, glaciers, more. Profusely illustrated. 240 black-and-white line drawings. 124 black-and-white photographs. 3 maps. Index. 576pp. 5⅜ × 8½. 25109-8 Pa. $11.95

THE BOOK OF BEASTS: Being a Translation from a Latin Bestiary of the Twelfth Century, T. H. White. Wonderful catalog real and fanciful beasts: manticore, griffin, phoenix, amphivius, jaculus, many more. White's witty erudite commentary on scientific, historical aspects. Fascinating glimpse of medieval mind. Illustrated. 296pp. 5⅜ × 8¼. (Available in U.S. only) 24609-4 Pa. $5.95

FRANK LLOYD WRIGHT: ARCHITECTURE AND NATURE With 160 Illustrations, Donald Hoffmann. Profusely illustrated study of influence of nature—especially prairie—on Wright's designs for Fallingwater, Robie House, Guggenheim Museum, other masterpieces. 96pp. 9¼ × 10¾. 25098-9 Pa. $7.95

FRANK LLOYD WRIGHT'S FALLINGWATER, Donald Hoffmann. Wright's famous waterfall house: planning and construction of organic idea. History of site, owners, Wright's personal involvement. Photographs of various stages of building. Preface by Edgar Kaufmann, Jr. 100 illustrations. 112pp. 9¼ × 10.
23671-4 Pa. $7.95

YEARS WITH FRANK LLOYD WRIGHT: Apprentice to Genius, Edgar Tafel. Insightful memoir by a former apprentice presents a revealing portrait of Wright the man, the inspired teacher, the greatest American architect. 372 black-and-white illustrations. Preface. Index. vi + 228pp. 8¼ × 11. 24801-1 Pa. $9.95

THE STORY OF KING ARTHUR AND HIS KNIGHTS, Howard Pyle. Enchanting version of King Arthur fable has delighted generations with imaginative narratives of exciting adventures and unforgettable illustrations by the author. 41 illustrations. xviii + 313pp. 6⅛ × 9¼. 21445-1 Pa. $5.95

THE GODS OF THE EGYPTIANS, E. A. Wallis Budge. Thorough coverage of numerous gods of ancient Egypt by foremost Egyptologist. Information on evolution of cults, rites and gods; the cult of Osiris; the Book of the Dead and its rites; the sacred animals and birds; Heaven and Hell; and more. 956pp. 6⅛ × 9¼.
22055-9, 22056-7 Pa., Two-vol. set $21.90

A THEOLOGICO-POLITICAL TREATISE, Benedict Spinoza. Also contains unfinished *Political Treatise*. Great classic on religious liberty, theory of government on common consent. R. Elwes translation. Total of 421pp. 5⅜ × 8½.
20249-6 Pa. $6.95

INCIDENTS OF TRAVEL IN CENTRAL AMERICA, CHIAPAS, AND YUCATAN, John L. Stephens. Almost single-handed discovery of Maya culture; exploration of ruined cities, monuments, temples; customs of Indians. 115 drawings. 892pp. 5⅜ × 8½. 22404-X, 22405-8 Pa., Two-vol. set $15.90

LOS CAPRICHOS, Francisco Goya. 80 plates of wild, grotesque monsters and caricatures. Prado manuscript included. 183pp. 6⅝ × 9⅝. 22384-1 Pa. $4.95

AUTOBIOGRAPHY: The Story of My Experiments with Truth, Mohandas K. Gandhi. Not hagiography, but Gandhi in his own words. Boyhood, legal studies, purification, the growth of the Satyagraha (nonviolent protest) movement. Critical, inspiring work of the man who freed India. 480pp. 5⅜ × 8½. (Available in U.S. only)
24593-4 Pa. $6.95

ILLUSTRATED DICTIONARY OF HISTORIC ARCHITECTURE, edited by Cyril M. Harris. Extraordinary compendium of clear, concise definitions for over 5,000 important architectural terms complemented by over 2,000 line drawings. Covers full spectrum of architecture from ancient ruins to 20th-century Modernism. Preface. 592pp. 7½ × 9⅜. 24444-X Pa. $14.95

THE NIGHT BEFORE CHRISTMAS, Clement Moore. Full text, and woodcuts from original 1848 book. Also critical, historical material. 19 illustrations. 40pp. 4⅝ × 6. 22797-9 Pa. $2.50

THE LESSON OF JAPANESE ARCHITECTURE: 165 Photographs, Jiro Harada. Memorable gallery of 165 photographs taken in the 1930's of exquisite Japanese homes of the well-to-do and historic buildings. 13 line diagrams. 192pp. 8⅜ × 11¼. 24778-3 Pa. $8.95

THE AUTOBIOGRAPHY OF CHARLES DARWIN AND SELECTED LETTERS, edited by Francis Darwin. The fascinating life of eccentric genius composed of an intimate memoir by Darwin (intended for his children); commentary by his son, Francis; hundreds of fragments from notebooks, journals, papers; and letters to and from Lyell, Hooker, Huxley, Wallace and Henslow. xi + 365pp. 5⅜ × 8. 20479-0 Pa. $5.95

WONDERS OF THE SKY: Observing Rainbows, Comets, Eclipses, the Stars and Other Phenomena, Fred Schaaf. Charming, easy-to-read poetic guide to all manner of celestial events visible to the naked eye. Mock suns, glories, Belt of Venus, more. Illustrated. 299pp. 5¼ × 8¼. 24402-4 Pa. $7.95

BURNHAM'S CELESTIAL HANDBOOK, Robert Burnham, Jr. Thorough guide to the stars beyond our solar system. Exhaustive treatment. Alphabetical by constellation: Andromeda to Cetus in Vol. 1; Chamaeleon to Orion in Vol. 2; and Pavo to Vulpecula in Vol. 3. Hundreds of illustrations. Index in Vol. 3. 2,000pp. 6⅛ × 9¼. 23567-X, 23568-8, 23673-0 Pa., Three-vol. set $37.85

STAR NAMES: Their Lore and Meaning, Richard Hinckley Allen. Fascinating history of names various cultures have given to constellations and literary and folkloristic uses that have been made of stars. Indexes to subjects. Arabic and Greek names. Biblical references. Bibliography. 563pp. 5⅜ × 8½. 21079-0 Pa. $7.95

THIRTY YEARS THAT SHOOK PHYSICS: The Story of Quantum Theory, George Gamow. Lucid, accessible introduction to influential theory of energy and matter. Careful explanations of Dirac's anti-particles, Bohr's model of the atom, much more. 12 plates. Numerous drawings. 240pp. 5⅜ × 8½. 24895-X Pa. $4.95

CHINESE DOMESTIC FURNITURE IN PHOTOGRAPHS AND MEASURED DRAWINGS, Gustav Ecke. A rare volume, now affordably priced for antique collectors, furniture buffs and art historians. Detailed review of styles ranging from early Shang to late Ming. Unabridged republication. 161 black-and-white drawings, photos. Total of 224pp. 8⅜ × 11¼. (Available in U.S. only) 25171-3 Pa. $12.95

VINCENT VAN GOGH: A Biography, Julius Meier-Graefe. Dynamic, penetrating study of artist's life, relationship with brother, Theo, painting techniques, travels, more. Readable, engrossing. 160pp. 5⅜ × 8½. (Available in U.S. only) 25253-1 Pa. $3.95

HOW TO WRITE, Gertrude Stein. Gertrude Stein claimed anyone could understand her unconventional writing—here are clues to help. Fascinating improvisations, language experiments, explanations illuminate Stein's craft and the art of writing. Total of 414pp. 4⅝ × 6⅜. 23144-5 Pa. $5.95

ADVENTURES AT SEA IN THE GREAT AGE OF SAIL: Five Firsthand Narratives, edited by Elliot Snow. Rare true accounts of exploration, whaling, shipwreck, fierce natives, trade, shipboard life, more. 33 illustrations. Introduction. 353pp. 5⅜ × 8½. 25177-2 Pa. $7.95

THE HERBAL OR GENERAL HISTORY OF PLANTS, John Gerard. Classic descriptions of about 2,850 plants—with over 2,700 illustrations—includes Latin and English names, physical descriptions, varieties, time and place of growth, more. 2,706 illustrations. xlv + 1,678pp. 8½ × 12¼. 23147-X Cloth. $75.00

DOROTHY AND THE WIZARD IN OZ, L. Frank Baum. Dorothy and the Wizard visit the center of the Earth, where people are vegetables, glass houses grow and Oz characters reappear. Classic sequel to *Wizard of Oz*. 256pp. 5⅜ × 8. 24714-7 Pa. $4.95

SONGS OF EXPERIENCE: Facsimile Reproduction with 26 Plates in Full Color, William Blake. This facsimile of Blake's original "Illuminated Book" reproduces 26 full-color plates from a rare 1826 edition. Includes "The Tyger," "London," "Holy Thursday," and other immortal poems. 26 color plates. Printed text of poems. 48pp. 5¼ × 7. 24636-1 Pa. $3.50

SONGS OF INNOCENCE, William Blake. The first and most popular of Blake's famous "Illuminated Books," in a facsimile edition reproducing all 31 brightly colored plates. Additional printed text of each poem. 64pp. 5¼ × 7. 22764-2 Pa. $3.50

PRECIOUS STONES, Max Bauer. Classic, thorough study of diamonds, rubies, emeralds, garnets, etc.: physical character, occurrence, properties, use, similar topics. 20 plates, 8 in color. 94 figures. 659pp. 6⅛ × 9¼. 21910-0, 21911-9 Pa., Two-vol. set $15.90

ENCYCLOPEDIA OF VICTORIAN NEEDLEWORK, S. F. A. Caulfeild and Blanche Saward. Full, precise descriptions of stitches, techniques for dozens of needlecrafts—most exhaustive reference of its kind. Over 800 figures. Total of 679pp. 8⅛ × 11. Two volumes. Vol. 1 22800-2 Pa. $11.95
Vol. 2 22801-0 Pa. $11.95

THE MARVELOUS LAND OF OZ, L. Frank Baum. Second Oz book, the Scarecrow and Tin Woodman are back with hero named Tip, Oz magic. 136 illustrations. 287pp. 5⅜ × 8½. 20692-0 Pa. $5.95

WILD FOWL DECOYS, Joel Barber. Basic book on the subject, by foremost authority and collector. Reveals history of decoy making and rigging, place in American culture, different kinds of decoys, how to make them, and how to use them. 140 plates. 156pp. 7⅞ × 10¾. 20011-6 Pa. $8.95

HISTORY OF LACE, Mrs. Bury Palliser. Definitive, profusely illustrated chronicle of lace from earliest times to late 19th century. Laces of Italy, Greece, England, France, Belgium, etc. Landmark of needlework scholarship. 266 illustrations. 672pp. 6⅛ × 9¼. 24742-2 Pa. $14.95

ILLUSTRATED GUIDE TO SHAKER FURNITURE, Robert Meader. All furniture and appurtenances, with much on unknown local styles. 235 photos. 146pp. 9 × 12. 22819-3 Pa. $7.95

WHALE SHIPS AND WHALING: A Pictorial Survey, George Francis Dow. Over 200 vintage engravings, drawings, photographs of barks, brigs, cutters, other vessels. Also harpoons, lances, whaling guns, many other artifacts. Comprehensive text by foremost authority. 207 black-and-white illustrations. 288pp. 6 × 9. 24808-9 Pa. $8.95

THE BERTRAMS, Anthony Trollope. Powerful portrayal of blind self-will and thwarted ambition includes one of Trollope's most heartrending love stories. 497pp. 5⅜ × 8½. 25119-5 Pa. $8.95

ADVENTURES WITH A HAND LENS, Richard Headstrom. Clearly written guide to observing and studying flowers and grasses, fish scales, moth and insect wings, egg cases, buds, feathers, seeds, leaf scars, moss, molds, ferns, common crystals, etc.—all with an ordinary, inexpensive magnifying glass. 209 exact line drawings aid in your discoveries. 220pp. 5⅜ × 8½. 23330-8 Pa. $4.50

RODIN ON ART AND ARTISTS, Auguste Rodin. Great sculptor's candid, wide-ranging comments on meaning of art; great artists; relation of sculpture to poetry, painting, music; philosophy of life, more. 76 superb black-and-white illustrations of Rodin's sculpture, drawings and prints. 119pp. 8⅜ × 11¼. 24487-3 Pa. $6.95

FIFTY CLASSIC FRENCH FILMS, 1912–1982: A Pictorial Record, Anthony Slide. Memorable stills from Grand Illusion, Beauty and the Beast, Hiroshima, Mon Amour, many more. Credits, plot synopses, reviews, etc. 160pp. 8¼ × 11. 25256-6 Pa. $11.95

THE PRINCIPLES OF PSYCHOLOGY, William James. Famous long course complete, unabridged. Stream of thought, time perception, memory, experimental methods; great work decades ahead of its time. 94 figures. 1,391pp. 5⅜ × 8½. 20381-6, 20382-4 Pa., Two-vol. set $19.90

BODIES IN A BOOKSHOP, R. T. Campbell. Challenging mystery of blackmail and murder with ingenious plot and superbly drawn characters. In the best tradition of British suspense fiction. 192pp. 5⅜ × 8½. 24720-1 Pa. $3.95

CALLAS: PORTRAIT OF A PRIMA DONNA, George Jellinek. Renowned commentator on the musical scene chronicles incredible career and life of the most controversial, fascinating, influential operatic personality of our time. 64 black-and-white photographs. 416pp. 5⅜ × 8¼. 25047-4 Pa. $7.95

GEOMETRY, RELATIVITY AND THE FOURTH DIMENSION, Rudolph Rucker. Exposition of fourth dimension, concepts of relativity as Flatland characters continue adventures. Popular, easily followed yet accurate, profound. 141 illustrations. 133pp. 5⅜ × 8½. 23400-2 Pa. $3.50

HOUSEHOLD STORIES BY THE BROTHERS GRIMM, with pictures by Walter Crane. 53 classic stories—Rumpelstiltskin, Rapunzel, Hansel and Gretel, the Fisherman and his Wife, Snow White, Tom Thumb, Sleeping Beauty, Cinderella, and so much more—lavishly illustrated with original 19th century drawings. 114 illustrations. x + 269pp. 5⅜ × 8½. 21080-4 Pa. $4.50

SUNDIALS, Albert Waugh. Far and away the best, most thorough coverage of ideas, mathematics concerned, types, construction, adjusting anywhere. Over 100 illustrations. 230pp. 5⅜ × 8½. 22947-5 Pa. $4.50

PICTURE HISTORY OF THE NORMANDIE: With 190 Illustrations, Frank O. Braynard. Full story of legendary French ocean liner: Art Deco interiors, design innovations, furnishings, celebrities, maiden voyage, tragic fire, much more. Extensive text. 144pp. 8⅞ × 11¾. 25257-4 Pa. $9.95

THE FIRST AMERICAN COOKBOOK: A Facsimile of "American Cookery," 1796, Amelia Simmons. Facsimile of the first American-written cookbook published in the United States contains authentic recipes for colonial favorites—pumpkin pudding, winter squash pudding, spruce beer, Indian slapjacks, and more. Introductory Essay and Glossary of colonial cooking terms. 80pp. 5⅜ × 8½. 24710-4 Pa. $3.50

101 PUZZLES IN THOUGHT AND LOGIC, C. R. Wylie, Jr. Solve murders and robberies, find out which fishermen are liars, how a blind man could possibly identify a color—purely by your own reasoning! 107pp. 5⅜ × 8½. 20367-0 Pa. $2.50

THE BOOK OF WORLD-FAMOUS MUSIC—CLASSICAL, POPULAR AND FOLK, James J. Fuld. Revised and enlarged republication of landmark work in musico-bibliography. Full information about nearly 1,000 songs and compositions including first lines of music and lyrics. New supplement. Index. 800pp. 5⅜ × 8¼. 24857-7 Pa. $14.95

ANTHROPOLOGY AND MODERN LIFE, Franz Boas. Great anthropologist's classic treatise on race and culture. Introduction by Ruth Bunzel. Only inexpensive paperback edition. 255pp. 5⅜ × 8½. 25245-0 Pa. $5.95

THE TALE OF PETER RABBIT, Beatrix Potter. The inimitable Peter's terrifying adventure in Mr. McGregor's garden, with all 27 wonderful, full-color Potter illustrations. 55pp. 4¼ × 5½. (Available in U.S. only) 22827-4 Pa. $1.75

THREE PROPHETIC SCIENCE FICTION NOVELS, H. G. Wells. *When the Sleeper Wakes, A Story of the Days to Come* and *The Time Machine* (full version). 335pp. 5⅜ × 8½. (Available in U.S. only) 20605-X Pa. $5.95

APICIUS COOKERY AND DINING IN IMPERIAL ROME, edited and translated by Joseph Dommers Vehling. Oldest known cookbook in existence offers readers a clear picture of what foods Romans ate, how they prepared them, etc. 49 illustrations. 301pp. 6⅛ × 9¼. 23563-7 Pa. $6.50

SHAKESPEARE LEXICON AND QUOTATION DICTIONARY, Alexander Schmidt. Full definitions, locations, shades of meaning of every word in plays and poems. More than 50,000 exact quotations. 1,485pp. 6½ × 9¼. 22726-X, 22727-8 Pa., Two-vol. set $27.90

THE WORLD'S GREAT SPEECHES, edited by Lewis Copeland and Lawrence W. Lamm. Vast collection of 278 speeches from Greeks to 1970. Powerful and effective models; unique look at history. 842pp. 5⅜ × 8½. 20468-5 Pa. $11.95

PLANTS OF THE BIBLE, Harold N. Moldenke and Alma L. Moldenke. Standard reference to all 230 plants mentioned in Scriptures. Latin name, biblical reference, uses, modern identity, much more. Unsurpassed encyclopedic resource for scholars, botanists, nature lovers, students of Bible. Bibliography. Indexes. 123 black-and-white illustrations. 384pp. 6 × 9. 25069-5 Pa. $8.95

FAMOUS AMERICAN WOMEN: A Biographical Dictionary from Colonial Times to the Present, Robert McHenry, ed. From Pocahontas to Rosa Parks, 1,035 distinguished American women documented in separate biographical entries. Accurate, up-to-date data, numerous categories, spans 400 years. Indices. 493pp. 6½ × 9¼. 24523-3 Pa. $9.95

THE FABULOUS INTERIORS OF THE GREAT OCEAN LINERS IN HISTORIC PHOTOGRAPHS, William H. Miller, Jr. Some 200 superb photographs capture exquisite interiors of world's great "floating palaces"—1890's to 1980's: *Titanic, Ile de France, Queen Elizabeth, United States, Europa*, more. Approx. 200 black-and-white photographs. Captions. Text. Introduction. 160pp. 8⅜ × 11¼. 24756-2 Pa. $9.95

THE GREAT LUXURY LINERS, 1927-1954: A Photographic Record, William H. Miller, Jr. Nostalgic tribute to heyday of ocean liners. 186 photos of Ile de France, Normandie, Leviathan, Queen Elizabeth, United States, many others. Interior and exterior views. Introduction. Captions. 160pp. 9 × 12. 24056-8 Pa. $9.95

A NATURAL HISTORY OF THE DUCKS, John Charles Phillips. Great landmark of ornithology offers complete detailed coverage of nearly 200 species and subspecies of ducks: gadwall, sheldrake, merganser, pintail, many more. 74 full-color plates, 102 black-and-white. Bibliography. Total of 1,920pp. 8⅜ × 11¼. 25141-1, 25142-X Cloth. Two-vol. set $100.00

THE SEAWEED HANDBOOK: An Illustrated Guide to Seaweeds from North Carolina to Canada, Thomas F. Lee. Concise reference covers 78 species. Scientific and common names, habitat, distribution, more. Finding keys for easy identification. 224pp. 5⅜ × 8½. 25215-9 Pa. $5.95

THE TEN BOOKS OF ARCHITECTURE: The 1755 Leoni Edition, Leon Battista Alberti. Rare classic helped introduce the glories of ancient architecture to the Renaissance. 68 black-and-white plates. 336pp. 8⅜ × 11¼. 25239-6 Pa. $14.95

MISS MACKENZIE, Anthony Trollope. Minor masterpieces by Victorian master unmasks many truths about life in 19th-century England. First inexpensive edition in years. 392pp. 5⅜ × 8½. 25201-9 Pa. $7.95

THE RIME OF THE ANCIENT MARINER, Gustave Doré, Samuel Taylor Coleridge. Dramatic engravings considered by many to be his greatest work. The terrifying space of the open sea, the storms and whirlpools of an unknown ocean, the ice of Antarctica, more—all rendered in a powerful, chilling manner. Full text. 38 plates. 77pp. 9¼ × 12. 22305-1 Pa. $4.95

THE EXPEDITIONS OF ZEBULON MONTGOMERY PIKE, Zebulon Montgomery Pike. Fascinating first-hand accounts (1805-6) of exploration of Mississippi River, Indian wars, capture by Spanish dragoons, much more. 1,088pp. 5⅜ × 8½. 25254-X, 25255-8 Pa. Two-vol. set $23.90

A CONCISE HISTORY OF PHOTOGRAPHY: Third Revised Edition, Helmut Gernsheim. Best one-volume history—camera obscura, photochemistry, daguerreotypes, evolution of cameras, film, more. Also artistic aspects—landscape, portraits, fine art, etc. 281 black-and-white photographs. 26 in color. 176pp. 8⅜ × 11¼. 25128-4 Pa. $12.95

THE DORÉ BIBLE ILLUSTRATIONS, Gustave Doré. 241 detailed plates from the Bible: the Creation scenes, Adam and Eve, Flood, Babylon, battle sequences, life of Jesus, etc. Each plate is accompanied by the verses from the King James version of the Bible. 241pp. 9 × 12. 23004-X Pa. $8.95

HUGGER-MUGGER IN THE LOUVRE, Elliot Paul. Second Homer Evans mystery-comedy. Theft at the Louvre involves sleuth in hilarious, madcap caper. "A knockout."—Books. 336pp. 5⅜ × 8½. 25185-3 Pa. $5.95

FLATLAND, E. A. Abbott. Intriguing and enormously popular science-fiction classic explores the complexities of trying to survive as a two-dimensional being in a three-dimensional world. Amusingly illustrated by the author. 16 illustrations. 103pp. 5⅜ × 8½. 20001-9 Pa. $2.25

THE HISTORY OF THE LEWIS AND CLARK EXPEDITION, Meriwether Lewis and William Clark, edited by Elliott Coues. Classic edition of Lewis and Clark's day-by-day journals that later became the basis for U.S. claims to Oregon and the West. Accurate and invaluable geographical, botanical, biological, meteorological and anthropological material. Total of 1,508pp. 5⅜ × 8½.
21268-8, 21269-6, 21270-X Pa. Three-vol. set $25.50

LANGUAGE, TRUTH AND LOGIC, Alfred J. Ayer. Famous, clear introduction to Vienna, Cambridge schools of Logical Positivism. Role of philosophy, elimination of metaphysics, nature of analysis, etc. 160pp. 5⅜ × 8½. (Available in U.S. and Canada only) 20010-8 Pa. $2.95

MATHEMATICS FOR THE NONMATHEMATICIAN, Morris Kline. Detailed, college-level treatment of mathematics in cultural and historical context, with numerous exercises. For liberal arts students. Preface. Recommended Reading Lists. Tables. Index. Numerous black-and-white figures. xvi + 641pp. 5⅜ × 8½.
24823-2 Pa. $11.95

28 SCIENCE FICTION STORIES, H. G. Wells. Novels, *Star Begotten* and *Men Like Gods,* plus 26 short stories: "Empire of the Ants," "A Story of the Stone Age," "The Stolen Bacillus," "In the Abyss," etc. 915pp. 5⅜ × 8½. (Available in U.S. only)
20265-8 Cloth. $10.95

HANDBOOK OF PICTORIAL SYMBOLS, Rudolph Modley. 3,250 signs and symbols, many systems in full; official or heavy commercial use. Arranged by subject. Most in Pictorial Archive series. 143pp. 8⅛ × 11. 23357-X Pa. $5.95

INCIDENTS OF TRAVEL IN YUCATAN, John L. Stephens. Classic (1843) exploration of jungles of Yucatan, looking for evidences of Maya civilization. Travel adventures, Mexican and Indian culture, etc. Total of 669pp. 5⅜ × 8½.
20926-1, 20927-X Pa., Two-vol. set $9.90

DEGAS: An Intimate Portrait, Ambroise Vollard. Charming, anecdotal memoir by famous art dealer of one of the greatest 19th-century French painters. 14 black-and-white illustrations. Introduction by Harold L. Van Doren. 96pp. 5⅜ × 8½.
25131-4 Pa. $3.95

PERSONAL NARRATIVE OF A PILGRIMAGE TO ALMANDINAH AND MECCAH, Richard Burton. Great travel classic by remarkably colorful personality. Burton, disguised as a Moroccan, visited sacred shrines of Islam, narrowly escaping death. 47 illustrations. 959pp. 5⅜ × 8½. 21217-3, 21218-1 Pa., Two-vol. set $17.90

PHRASE AND WORD ORIGINS, A. H. Holt. Entertaining, reliable, modern study of more than 1,200 colorful words, phrases, origins and histories. Much unexpected information. 254pp. 5⅜ × 8½. 20758-7 Pa. $5.95

THE RED THUMB MARK, R. Austin Freeman. In this first Dr. Thorndyke case, the great scientific detective draws fascinating conclusions from the nature of a single fingerprint. Exciting story, authentic science. 320pp. 5⅜ × 8½. (Available in U.S. only) 25210-8 Pa. $5.95

AN EGYPTIAN HIEROGLYPHIC DICTIONARY, E. A. Wallis Budge. Monumental work containing about 25,000 words or terms that occur in texts ranging from 3000 B.C. to 600 A.D. Each entry consists of a transliteration of the word, the word in hieroglyphs, and the meaning in English. 1,314pp. 6⅜ × 10.
23615-3, 23616-1 Pa., Two-vol. set $27.90

THE COMPLEAT STRATEGYST: Being a Primer on the Theory of Games of Strategy, J. D. Williams. Highly entertaining classic describes, with many illustrated examples, how to select best strategies in conflict situations. Prefaces. Appendices. xvi + 268pp. 5⅜ × 8½. 25101-2 Pa. $5.95

THE ROAD TO OZ, L. Frank Baum. Dorothy meets the Shaggy Man, little Button-Bright and the Rainbow's beautiful daughter in this delightful trip to the magical Land of Oz. 272pp. 5⅜ × 8. 25208-6 Pa. $4.95

POINT AND LINE TO PLANE, Wassily Kandinsky. Seminal exposition of role of point, line, other elements in non-objective painting. Essential to understanding 20th-century art. 127 illustrations. 192pp. 6½ × 9¼. 23808-3 Pa. $4.50

LADY ANNA, Anthony Trollope. Moving chronicle of Countess Lovel's bitter struggle to win for herself and daughter Anna their rightful rank and fortune—perhaps at cost of sanity itself. 384pp. 5⅜ × 8½. 24669-8 Pa. $6.95

EGYPTIAN MAGIC, E. A. Wallis Budge. Sums up all that is known about magic in Ancient Egypt: the role of magic in controlling the gods, powerful amulets that warded off evil spirits, scarabs of immortality, use of wax images, formulas and spells, the secret name, much more. 253pp. 5⅜ × 8½. 22681-6 Pa. $4.50

THE DANCE OF SIVA, Ananda Coomaraswamy. Preeminent authority unfolds the vast metaphysic of India: the revelation of her art, conception of the universe, social organization, etc. 27 reproductions of art masterpieces. 192pp. 5⅜ × 8½.
24817-8 Pa. $5.95

AMERICAN CLIPPER SHIPS: 1833–1858, Octavius T. Howe & Frederick C. Matthews. Fully-illustrated, encyclopedic review of 352 clipper ships from the period of America's greatest maritime supremacy. Introduction. 109 halftones. 5 black-and-white line illustrations. Index. Total of 928pp. 5⅜ × 8½.
25115-2, 25116-0 Pa., Two-vol. set $17.90

TOWARDS A NEW ARCHITECTURE, Le Corbusier. Pioneering manifesto by great architect, near legendary founder of "International School." Technical and aesthetic theories, views on industry, economics, relation of form to function, "mass-production spirit," much more. Profusely illustrated. Unabridged translation of 13th French edition. Introduction by Frederick Etchells. 320pp. 6⅛ × 9¼. (Available in U.S. only)
25023-7 Pa. $8.95

THE BOOK OF KELLS, edited by Blanche Cirker. Inexpensive collection of 32 full-color, full-page plates from the greatest illuminated manuscript of the Middle Ages, painstakingly reproduced from rare facsimile edition. Publisher's Note. Captions. 32pp. 9⅜ × 12¼.
24345-1 Pa. $4.95

BEST SCIENCE FICTION STORIES OF H. G. WELLS, H. G. Wells. Full novel *The Invisible Man*, plus 17 short stories: "The Crystal Egg," "Aepyornis Island," "The Strange Orchid," etc. 303pp. 5⅜ × 8½. (Available in U.S. only)
21531-8 Pa. $4.95

AMERICAN SAILING SHIPS: Their Plans and History, Charles G. Davis. Photos, construction details of schooners, frigates, clippers, other sailcraft of 18th to early 20th centuries—plus entertaining discourse on design, rigging, nautical lore, much more. 137 black-and-white illustrations. 240pp. 6⅛ × 9¼.
24658-2 Pa. $5.95

ENTERTAINING MATHEMATICAL PUZZLES, Martin Gardner. Selection of author's favorite conundrums involving arithmetic, money, speed, etc., with lively commentary. Complete solutions. 112pp. 5⅜ × 8½.
25211-6 Pa. $2.95

THE WILL TO BELIEVE, HUMAN IMMORTALITY, William James. Two books bound together. Effect of irrational on logical, and arguments for human immortality. 402pp. 5⅜ × 8½.
20291-7 Pa. $7.50

THE HAUNTED MONASTERY and THE CHINESE MAZE MURDERS, Robert Van Gulik. 2 full novels by Van Gulik continue adventures of Judge Dee and his companions. An evil Taoist monastery, seemingly supernatural events; overgrown topiary maze that hides strange crimes. Set in 7th-century China. 27 illustrations. 328pp. 5⅜ × 8½.
23502-5 Pa. $5.95

CELEBRATED CASES OF JUDGE DEE (DEE GOONG AN), translated by Robert Van Gulik. Authentic 18th-century Chinese detective novel; Dee and associates solve three interlocked cases. Led to Van Gulik's own stories with same characters. Extensive introduction. 9 illustrations. 237pp. 5⅜ × 8½.
23337-5 Pa. $4.95

Prices subject to change without notice.
Available at your book dealer or write for free catalog to Dept. GI, Dover Publications, Inc., 31 East 2nd St., Mineola, N.Y. 11501. Dover publishes more than 175 books each year on science, elementary and advanced mathematics, biology, music, art, literary history, social sciences and other areas.